Growing Your Own

COCKTAILS, MOCKTAILS, TEAS & INFUSIONS

Growing Your Own

COCKTAILS, MOCKTAILS, TEAS & INFUSIONS

GARDENING TIPS AND HOW-TO TECHNIQUES FOR MAKING ARTISANAL BEVERAGES AT HOME

JODI HELMER

WITH RECIPES BY JEANETTE HURT,
AUTHOR OF *DRINK LIKE A WOMAN*

Growing Your Own Cocktails, Mocktails, Teas & Infusions

CompanionHouse Books™ is an imprint of Fox Chapel Publishing.

Project Team
Editor: Colleen Dorsey
Copy Editor: Amy Deputato
Design: Mary Ann Kahn
Index: Jay Kreider

ISBN 978-1-62008-383-3

Library of Congress Control Number:2019955843

Fox Chapel Publishing
903 Square Street
Mount Joy, PA 17552

www.facebook.com/companionhousebooks

We are always looking for talented authors. To submit an idea,
please send a brief inquiry to acquisitions@foxchapelpublishing.com.

Printed and bound in Singapore
23 22 21 20   2 4 6 8 10 9 7 5 3 1

DEDICATION

For Dad. From my first Shirley Temple to your last double-double, our best conversations were always over a drink.

ACKNOWLEDGMENTS

Thanks to Bud Sperry at Fox Chapel Publishing for giving me another chance to turn an idea into a book and Colleen Dorsey for editing out nonsensical sentences, triple-checking for accuracy, and keeping the pages turning on time. Superstar cocktail writer and recipe developer Jeanette Hurt turned a list of plants into a lineup of must-drink cocktails; Kyle Edwards shared some great photos; and talented designer Beth Kaiser took basic garden design sketches and created stunning visuals to bring them to life.

To each person who shared a (real or virtual) drink with me during this journey—Megan Bame, Heather Rice Books, Polly Campbell, Jenny Fink, Kate Hanley, Wendy Helfenbaum, Beth Howard, Kelly James, Judi Ketteler, and Rosie Molinary—thank you for always offering support and a sip of whatever you're drinking. I also want to raise a glass to my family, Hank and Dianne Helmer, Shannon Helmer, Charlotte McKinnon, and Jerry Porter, who give me countless reasons to celebrate.

CONTENTS

INTRODUCTION ~ 8

CHAPTER 1:
BRIEF HISTORIES OF YOUR FAVORITE DRINKS ~ 12
Shaking Up Cocktail Culture, 14
A Local Tea Movement Is Brewing, 19

CHAPTER 2:
CHOOSING PLANTS FOR YOUR BEVERAGE GARDEN ~ 24
Leaves, 26
Flowers, 59
Fruits and Vegetables, 70
Roots, 87

CHAPTER 3:
MIXING UP THE BEST BEVERAGE GARDEN ~ 94
Best Practices, 96
Garden Designs, 101

CHAPTER 4:
FROM CULTIVATION TO CUP:
MAKING PERFECT DRINKS ~ 110
Preparation, 112
Preserving the Harvest, 119

CHAPTER 5:
SHAKEN, NOT STIRRED: RECIPES FOR THE PERFECT
GARDEN-TO-GLASS BEVERAGES ~ 122
Simple Syrups, 124
Shrubs, 126
Cocktails, 128
Alcohol-Free Drinks, 138

Plant Hardiness Zone Maps, 144
Resources, 148
About the Author, 149
Photo Credits, 149
Index, 151

PLANT INDEX

LEAVES

Anise hyssop (*Agastache foeniculum*) 26
Apple mint (*Mentha suaveolens*) 27
Bearberry (*Arctostaphylos uva-ursi*)..... 28
Bee balm (*Monarda fistulosa*) 29
Cardamom (*Elettaria cardamomum*)..... 30
Catnip (*Nepeta cataria*)............... 31
Chickweed (*Cerastium arvense*) 32
Chocolate mint
   (*Mentha* × *piperita* 'Chocolate') 33
Cilantro/Coriander
   (*Coriandrum sativum*) 34
Eucalyptus (*Eucalyptus perriniana*) 35
Fennel (*Foeniculum vulgare*) 36
Holy basil (*Ocimum sanctum*)......... 37
Lavender mint
   (*Mentha* × *piperita* 'Lavender') 38
Lemon balm (*Melissa officinalis*) 39
Lemongrass (*Cymbopogon citratus*)...... 40
Lemon verbena (*Aloysia citriodora*) 41
Marjoram (*Origanum majorana*)....... 42
Parsley (*Petroselinum crispum*) 43
Peppermint (*Mentha* × *piperita*)....... 44
Pineapple sage (*Salvia elegans*)........ 45
Rosemary (*Rosmarinus officinalis*) 46
Sage (*Salvia officinalis*) 47
Spearmint (*Mentha spicata*) 48
Stinging nettle (*Urtica dioica*)......... 49
St. John's wort (*Hypericum calycinum*) ... 50
Tea plant (*Camellia sinensis*).......... 51
Thyme (*Thymus vulgaris*)............. 56
Witch hazel (*Hamamelis virginiana*) 57
Yaupon (*Ilex vomitoria*) 58

FLOWERS

Calendula (*Calendula officinalis*)....... 59
Chamomile (*Matricaria recutita*) 60
Dandelion (*Taraxacum officinale*) 61

Echinacea (*Echinacea purpurea*)........ 62
Hibiscus (*Hibiscus rosa-sinensis*) 63
Jasmine (*Jasminum officinale*) 64
Lavender (*Lavandula angustifolia*) 65
Purple passionflower
   (*Passiflora incarnata*) 66
Red clover (*Trifolium pratense*) 67
Trumpet honeysuckle
   (*Lonicera sempervirens*) 68
Tufted violet (*Viola cornuta*)........... 69

FRUITS AND VEGETABLES

Beet (*Beta vulgaris*)................. 70
Blackberry (*Rubus* sp.)............... 71
Black currant (*Ribes nigrum*) 72
Blood orange (*Citrus* × *sinensis*)....... 73
Carrot (*Daucus carota* var. *sativus*) 74
Celery (*Apium graveolens*)............ 75
Cucumber (*Cucumis sativus*) 76
Kale (*Brassica oleracea*)............... 77
Meyer lemon (*Citrus* × *meyeri*) 78
Persimmon (*Diospyros virginiana*) 79
Raspberry (*Rubus idaeus*)............. 80
Rhubarb (*Rheum rhabarbarum*) 81
Rugosa rose (*Rosa rugosa*) 82
Spinach (*Spinacia oleracea*)........... 83
Staghorn sumac (*Rhus typhina*)....... 84
Strawberry (*Fragaria* × *ananassa*) 85
Tomato (*Solanum lycopersicum*) 86

ROOTS

Burdock (*Arctium lappa*) 87
Chicory (*Cichorium intybus*).......... 88
Ginger (*Zingiber officinale*) 89
Ginseng (*Panax quinquefolius*) 90
Licorice (*Glycyrrhiza glabra*).......... 91
Valerian (*Valeriana officinalis*) 92

INTRODUCTION

Exploring a garden center will give you many ideas for adding to your garden—some standard, some surprising.

Each season, I vow to go to the garden center with a plan: a list, some idea of what I want to grow, a realistic notion of how much space we have, how much we can eat in a season, and how we might use the ingredients in our kitchen. And, each season, the same thing happens: I abandon all logic the moment I see colorful seed packets and seedlings poking through the soil in small plastic pots. Who cares that I have never tried a cucamelon or grown lemongrass? The unusual finds end up in the cart alongside tried-and-true favorites, and it all ends up in the garden. When the plants mature, I scramble to find creative ways to use the bounty. For me, the most successful reimagining has been taking those ingredients from garden to glass.

As my garden grew beyond my original plans, the fruits, vegetables, and herbs

Sitting in your garden, surrounded by fresh ingredients you grew, is the best way to enjoy a garden-to-glass beverage.

growing outside my back door started finding their way not just onto our plates but also into our favorite—and most memorable—drinks. As it turns out, this wasn't just happening at our house. Garden to glass is a trend that is quickly catching on as gardeners (and mixologists) have looked beyond their plates and started incorporating their harvests into cocktails, mocktails, teas, infused waters, lemonades, juices, and other fresh, flavorful drinks. A beverage garden combines two of the things I love most: great drinks and a garden filled with the ingredients to make them.

The garden-to-glass trend started with cocktails. The National Restaurant Association has featured artisan spirits, including culinary cocktails made from fresh savory- or herb-infused ingredients, on its annual list of the hottest culinary trends for an entire decade. In 2019, Kimpton Hotels & Restaurants released its Culinary + Cocktail Trends Forecast, and in it bartenders listed "vegetable cocktails" as a strong (and growing) trend, citing plans to go beyond conventional cocktail ingredients like celery, cilantro, mint, and cucumber and incorporate more surprising vegetables such as endives, fiddleheads, tomatillos, mushrooms, and sunchokes into their drink menus. Mike Ryan, director of bars at Kimpton Hotels & Restaurants, explained, "A lot of these influences come directly from the kitchen. There might be a flavor profile a bartender loves in a particular dish, and he or she figures out how to bring that to life in a cocktail."

A mushroom cocktail is just one example of the flavor innovation that has been occurring in recent years.

Pairing the flavor profiles of a cocktail with a dish is a great challenge for modern chefs—and amateurs!

Even with limited space, you can use just your windowsill to start your own beverage garden.

The trend quickly expanded beyond cocktails. Mocktails, cocktail-like drinks made without alcohol, are an ever-expanding menu category, and more mixologists and home bartenders are skipping supermarket fruit juices and syrups for homemade versions, making ingredients with fresh harvests from their gardens. Even soda is being reformulated. A *USA Today* article on the trend notes that sales of carbonated soft drinks are flat, but craft sodas are capturing a "share by hyping premium and natural ingredients, creative flavors, limited runs, unusual packaging, or their local roots." Craft sodas, like other small-batch beverages, tend to use healthier ingredients and natural sweeteners such as agave nectar, stevia, and honey, which all start in the garden.

And, while it might seem daunting or fancy, growing the ingredients to make tea, infused water, cocktails, mocktails, lemonades, and other culinary beverages is actually a great project for both beginning and experienced gardeners. Fruits, vegetables, and herbs are often easy to grow (most will thrive in pots on a sun-drenched windowsill), and making a garden-to-glass drink can be super simple.

Your own beverage garden can be as basic as a raised bed with a handful of herbs or as elaborate as an entire landscape filled with fruits, vines, trees, and flowers that can be mixed, muddled, blended, shaken, and stirred into fabulous craft beverages.

When the time comes to harvest your bounty, you can stick with the basics—a few handfuls of vegetables in the blender for fresh vegetable juice; muddled strawberries and sugar for lemonade; or mint leaves steeped in boiling water for tea that tastes better than anything you can buy in a store. Or you can take your mixology skills to the next level, turning up the flavor on basic cocktails like mojitos and sangria by using just-picked ingredients from your custom beverage garden. You can even make your own simple syrups and shrubs—the building blocks of popular craft beverages—with your garden bounty. (Never heard of shrub? See page 126!)

Whether you've never tended to a plant or already have a large garden and want a new hobby, starting a beverage garden and sipping refreshing and delicious concoctions is a great way to add a punch of flavor to your favorite drinks or experiment with new favorites. You'll soon find yourself planning an entire garden around ingredients you can eat *and* drink.

Read the plant descriptions and see what appeals to you (and your growing conditions); check out the sample garden designs for inspiration; and experiment with the recipes to discover new favorite drinks. Whether you grow a handful of plants for one go-to beverage or decide to fill your garden with edibles to make all of your drinks from scratch, the goal is to have fun sampling the bounty of cocktails, mocktails, teas, and infusions that you can make from plants growing in your garden.

Go as deep into mixology as you wish—even the advanced stuff only requires a small set of tools.

Disclaimer: This book is not a field guide; it's not intended to diagnose, treat, or cure any disease. I am a gardener, not a doctor or nutritionist. Although I did extensive research to ensure accuracy, you must make sure to positively identify all plants before eating leaves, flowers, fruits, and roots. Some wild plants are poisonous or can have adverse effects. Avoid consuming any unfamiliar plants. Consult with qualified health professionals to verify the health benefits and safety of consuming plants.

Chapter 1

BRIEF HISTORIES OF YOUR FAVORITE DRINKS

Every drink has a story. Whether you prefer herbal teas, craft sodas, flavored waters, or classic cocktails, the beverages you drink today have evolved since they were first brewed, sipped, shaken, or stirred. In this chapter, we'll focus on two general categories of drinks: cocktails and tea.

Shaking Up Cocktail Culture

Traditional cocktails were simple: mix spirits, sugar, water, and bitters—known as a bitter sling—and sip. A 1798 article in the British newspaper *The Morning Post and Gazetteer* was believed to be the first to mention the word "cocktail," but the practice of drinking spirits mixed with medicinal botanicals was common long before. Doctors often prescribed bitters made from herbs, fruits, flowers, bark, and roots believed to have medicinal properties to cure a range of ailments, infused in spirits such as gin. Although the earliest definition of *cocktails* (used in the 1862 book *How to Mix Drinks*) was limited to alcoholic drinks containing bitters (and not punches, sours, and toddies), it didn't take long before cocktails were defined as all mixed drinks made with a combination of alcohol and mixers like soda and fruit juices.

A Manhattan is an example of a cocktail that was developed during the golden age of cocktails, before Prohibition (which was from 1920–1933).

During Prohibition, the seizure and disposal of alcohol by federal agents was common.

Most of the drinks we see on bar menus today, including the daiquiri, martini, old fashioned, and Manhattan, were introduced between the 1860s and 1920, when Prohibition began, mixologist and cocktail historian Derek Brown said on a 2019 episode of *All Things Considered* on NPR. This so-called golden age of cocktails saw bartenders experimenting with different recipes, creating some of the drinks we now consider classics.

Adding mixers to cocktails became more important during Prohibition because the quality of illicit spirits was poor. Adding honey, fruit juice, and soda helped mask the flavor and made cocktails more palatable.

In recent years, social media has driven bartenders and restaurants to increasingly compete not only for great-tasting but also great-looking cocktails.

Cocktails have come a long way since the days of bathtub gin, however. Although the craft cocktail movement has been going strong for two decades, the local food movement has intensified the demand for small-batch spirits, increased the growth of farm distilleries, and upped the competition to create cocktails worthy of Instagram.

The United States now has more than 1,500 craft distilleries, up from just 68 in 2004, and a growing number are farm distilleries that grow their own fruits and grains or source them from local farms to produce artisanal spirits, according to the American Distilling Institute. Fans of the so-called grain-to-glass movement believe that using local, seasonal ingredients has a positive effect on the taste of distilled spirits and that using crops grown onsite allows distillers to create rum, gin, vodka, and whiskey that reflect the unique flavors of the region.

Rather than mixing craft spirits with mass-produced mixers, bartenders have embraced local ingredients. Restaurants

The US distillery scene has grown by leaps and bounds in just the last two decades.

Restaurants with kitchen gardens can market their garden-to-glass drinks.

Mixing Craft Cocktails at Home

If fancy mixed drinks are your tipple of choice, there's no need to leave the house to imbibe. Craft cocktails are now coming to your mailbox.

As meal kits have gained market share, cocktail subscription boxes have followed. The concept is similar: just as companies like Blue Apron curate all of the ingredients for make-at-home meals, companies offering cocktail subscription kits assemble and ship kits containing all of the ingredients for craft cocktails straight to your door.

Each subscription service has a different take on the model. Some deliver mini bottles of alcohol—just enough to make the featured recipe—while others ship craft cocktail ingredients with full-sized bottles of spirits to help you build your home bar. For subscribers, the kits are about more than the fixings for creative cocktails; they are educational, helping tipplers master the art of bartending.

in cities ranging from New York and San Francisco to Indianapolis and Las Vegas have even planted onsite gardens to harvest fresh fruits and herbs such as mint, basil, lavender, rosemary, and strawberries to use in their craft cocktails.

Cocktail enthusiasts are also looking to build their bartending skills. Paul Clarke, editor of *Imbibe* magazine, told attendees at the 2016 Chicago Cocktail Summit that we are living in the golden age of at-home mixology.

The craft cocktail revolution has also led to the rise of the mocktail movement. A portmanteau of "mock" and "cocktail,"

Mocktail culture has come a long way since the days of simple Shirley Temples.

The Evolution of Mixers

Mixed drinks made with spirits and soda or a splash of water will always be popular. Craft sodas and flavored water have replaced big brands and bottled water as popular mixers for cocktails and mocktails. The global flavored water market reached $10.3 billion in 2018, with sales in the United States alone almost doubling between 2013 and 2018, according to Euromonitor International, and the market for craft sodas is expected to top $840 million by 2024. Flavors such as orange mango, blackberry cucumber, and strawberry watermelon—which can all be made with fruits and vegetables growing in your garden—were the top flavor combinations.

mocktails have all of the sophistication and flavor of craft cocktails with none of the alcohol. In May 2019, Distill Ventures released a study that found 61 percent of drinkers in the United Kingdom wanted better choices in nonalcoholic drinks. The study also noted that 83 percent of bar managers in Los Angeles called no-proof drinks a growing trend.

Online food magazine *Eater* declared, "Virgin drinks are growing up," noting that the mocktail revolution has made the Shirley Temple and virgin piña coladas obsolete and created demand for garden-to-glass ingredients used in shrubs and bitters. Sylvie Gabriele, owner of Love & Salt restaurant in Manhattan, told the magazine, "In some ways, [mocktails] take more development than an alcoholic drink. Alcohol by nature has a body and a kick, and we had to really develop these flavor profiles to produce a full experience [in our mocktails]."

Whether you order a craft mocktail from the bar or mix up a pitcher of mojitos to sip outside on a summer night, using freshly harvested ingredients adds an extra punch of flavor that turns a drink into an experience.

A Local Tea Movement Is Brewing

Tea has been cultivated for centuries, with the earliest records dating back to 2732 BC, when, according to legend, Emperor Shen Nung first drank tea after leaves from a *Camellia sinensis* bush—that is, the tea plant—drifted

De Materia Medica has been published in many languages throughout the centuries, but it always contained useful information about helpful plants—including tea.

into his pot of boiling water. More reliable records show that tea was included in the medical text *De Materia Medica*, which was first published around 200 BC.

As tea started becoming more popular as a drink, not just a medicine, the cultivation, harvesting, and processing of *Camellia sinensis* started. During the Tang Dynasty (618–906 AD), often referred to as the classic age of tea, the botanical beverage became known as the national drink of China; tea was sipped and savored from the Imperial Palace to rural villages. Tea also became the centerpiece of spiritual rituals. During the Tang Dynasty, Buddhist monk Lu Yu wrote *Ch'a Ching*, a tea treatise that centered Buddhist, Taoist, and Confucian teachings around traditional tea ceremonies.

Toward the end of the seventeenth century, camel trains operating along the Silk Road transported tea between China and Russia. In 1610, the Dutch East India Company brought the first shipments of tea to Europe. Tea was first served to the public in 1657. Thanks to its high price, it was

At first, tea was expensive and therefore only enjoyed by the rich.

enjoyed only by the royal and aristocratic classes. It wasn't until one hundred years after the first tea was imported to England that teahouses and tea gardens started popping up around London and tea became the national drink of the British Isles. So, while England might have a well-deserved reputation for serving high tea, the British were actually late adopters of tea culture.

Dutch settlers also brought tea to America. The upper class who settled in New Amsterdam, later renamed New York, started drinking tea in the 1600s. The British East India Company secured a monopoly on tea sales in the American colonies after British parliament passed the Tea Act on May 10, 1773. The legislation

What Is a Tisane?

Some of the most popular "teas" are not tea at all. True tea is made from the leaves of the *Camellia sinensis* plant; herbal teas, including popular brews such as chamomile and peppermint, are considered tisanes.

Tisanes (pronounced ti-ZAN) are made from ingredients such as herbs, flowers, fruits, bark, and roots but no white, green, black, or oolong teas. (The French word for "herbal infusion" is *tisane*.) Rooibos (pronounced ROY-boss), also known as African red tea or red bush tea (because it's made from a South African rooibos plant), and yerba maté (pronounced YER-ba MAH-tay), a South American botanical drink brewed from a plant in the holly family, are also considered tisanes.

Unlike true tea brewed from *Camellia sinensis* leaves, which contain up to 90 milligrams of caffeine per 8-ounce (240ml) cup, tisanes are caffeine free. These teas, also called infusions or botanicals, can be sipped hot or iced.

Iconic in American history, the Boston Tea Party treated tea as a symbol of oppression.

angered colonists, and, on December 16, 1773, a group calling themselves the Sons of Liberty boarded ships anchored in the Boston Harbor and dumped 92,000 pounds of tea into the water. The event came to be known as the Boston Tea Party.

Pressure from independent tea merchants like Richard Twining uncovered corruption within the British East India Company and put pressure on the British government to end the monopoly on the tea trade. The campaign was successful, and the British East India Company folded in 1874, opening the door for America to import tea directly from China. Clipper ships began transporting the commodity across the ocean.

Twinings, founded by an independent family of tea merchants who ultimately helped end the monopoly on the tea trade, remains one of the most successful and iconic British tea brands today.

The rolling, stepped hills of Chinese tea plantations are where the most tea is produced in the world.

Worldwide, China still dominates tea production, harvesting more than 1.8 million tons of tea each year. Other top tea-producing countries include India, Kenya, Sri Lanka, and Indonesia. The United States might not be a top cultivator of *Camellia sinensis*, but it is a significant importer.

Approximately 80 percent of Americans are tea drinkers. Thanks to strong demand, US growers are experimenting with the crop and producing small-batch, artisanal teas with some success. The Charleston Tea Plantation in Charleston, South Carolina, has been growing tea since 1987 and was the sole commercial tea grower in the nation for many years. Now, the US League of Tea Growers reports that there are sixty farms in fifteen states growing *Camellia sinensis*. Most, including Table Rock Tea Company, The Great Mississippi Tea Co., and Virginia First Tea Farm, were started within the last ten years.

Tea grown in the United States is more expensive. Labor costs are much higher than in traditional tea-producing countries, where growers might earn less than $20 per week, making domestic tea

A massive quantity of leaves is required to produce tea.

a high-end artisanal product. Compared to supermarket tea bags, which can retail for as little as $2.50 for 100 bags of black or green tea, loose-leaf tea grown and processed in the United States can cost as much as $1 per gram. (It takes about 2.5 grams of loose-leaf tea to brew a single cup.) The sheer rarity of US-grown tea justifies the high price, according to the US League of Tea Growers.

Teas and infusions are incredibly popular in the United States, with a large variety available on standard supermarket shelves.

Chapter 2

CHOOSING PLANTS FOR YOUR BEVERAGE GARDEN

The best thing about growing leaves, flowers, fruits, vegetables, and roots to use in your favorite drinks is that there are no rules and no list of plants that "should" be included. Get creative! Choose plants based on their flavors or health benefits or aesthetic appeal; experiment with new plants; remove plants that aren't working for you. Fill your garden with plants you love, and enjoy sipping and sharing your garden-to-glass drinks.

What Plant Hardiness Zone Do I Live In?

The US Department of Agriculture (USDA) established a Plant Hardiness Zone Map to help gardeners determine which plants would grow best in their locations. The map divides the nation into thirteen distinct growing zones, with each zone subdivided into "a" and "b" categories, based on average minimum winter temperatures. In the coldest zone, zone 1a, which includes Alaska, minimum winter temperatures range from -60°F to -55°F (-51°C to -48°C); in zone 13b, the island of Puerto Rico, average minimum winter temperatures range from 65°F to 70°F (18°C to 21°C). Cultivate outdoor plants that suit your zone, or cultivate other plants indoors or in a greenhouse. You will find a full-size reproduction of this zone map on pages 144–147.

Leaves

ANISE HYSSOP
(*Agastache foeniculum*)

■ ZONES: 4 TO 8

This herbaceous perennial bursts into bloom from June to September. Its tight spikes of lavender to purple flowers provide nectar that attracts butterflies and hummingbirds, earning it the nickname "hummingbird mint." In a beverage garden, its foliage is the main attraction. As its name suggests, anise hyssop produces fragrant leaves with a strong anise (licorice) flavor.

Native Americans prized anise hyssop for its medicinal uses. Thanks to its antibacterial and anti-inflammatory properties, the herb, also known as blue giant, has been used to relieve congestion, reduce fevers, ease coughing, and alleviate diarrhea.

The light green, heart-shaped leaves can be plucked straight from the plant and added to your favorite beverages. You can also use the dried leaves and flowers to make a range of drinks from hot and iced tea to cocktails.

Anise hyssop is native to North America and grows well in sun to part shade. Although it tolerates most soil conditions, it requires good drainage to thrive. The clumping perennial grows up to 4 feet (1.2m) tall and 1 to 3 feet (30 to 90cm) wide. A member of the mint family, anise hyssop spreads via rhizomes and will aggressively self-seed; consider planting it in containers to keep it from taking over the garden.

 In Your Glass:

Use anise hyssop in hot or iced tea and cocktails and mocktails, especially those made with mint, peaches, and lavender. Mix ¼ cup (60ml) of anise hyssop leaves, 1 cup (240ml) of sugar, and 1 cup (240ml) of water to make lemonade.

APPLE MINT
(*Mentha suaveolens*)
■ **ZONES:** 5 TO 9

Apple mint is a fast-growing ground cover with rounded leaves. Thanks to the fine hairs covering its leaves, apple mint earned the nickname "woolly mint." Despite being part of the mint family, apple mint has a fruity fragrance and a hint of apple flavor; it's less minty than other kinds of mint.

An aggressive spreader, apple mint grows up to 2 feet (60cm) tall and just as wide. Pruning the rhizomes helps control the spread; planting apple mint in pots will also keep it from taking over the garden. Choose a location in full sun to part shade and keep the soil moist. Cut the flower spikes after the pink or white flowers bloom in July and August to stimulate new growth.

Pineapple mint (*Mentha suaveolens* 'Variegata') is a subspecies of apple mint and has variegated foliage that makes it distinct from other mint species. The leaves have a strong fragrance and sweet citrus-mint flavor. To maintain the attractive green-and-white leaves, prune all of the pure green leaves, which will take over if allowed. White or light pink flowers blossom in July and August, attracting pollinating insects. Like its parent plant, pineapple mint grows up to 2 feet (60cm) tall and prefers full sun to part shade and moist soil. It's also a vigorous spreader.

Both apple and pineapple mint contain vitamins A and C, calcium, iron, and potassium. Both are used for ailments ranging from indigestion to headaches.

 *In Your Glass:*

Add 1 cup (240ml) of apple (or pineapple) mint leaves or ½ cup (120ml) of dried leaves to 2 cups (480ml) of boiling water to make delicious hot tea. Both fruit-flavored mint varieties taste great in a whiskey-based iced tea. Other mints, like spearmint or peppermint, or fruit-flavored herbs, like pineapple sage, complement the flavors of both apple mint and pineapple mint tea.

BEARBERRY

(*Arctostaphylos uva-ursi*)

■ **ZONES:** 2 TO 7

Though bearberry gets its name for the clusters of berries that attract hungry bears, in a beverage garden, this evergreen shrub is prized for its leaves, stems, and roots, not its fruit.

Native to northern regions in the United States, Canada, Europe, and Asia, bearberry is hardy enough to survive severe winters and will struggle in hot and humid climates. In the right climate, though, bearberry is easy to grow. Plant it in full sun and acidic, well-drained soil. Once established, bearberry is drought tolerant. A mature shrub will grow just 1 foot (30cm) high and spread up to 6 feet (1.8m) wide. The white to light pink flowers bloom in April and May, and fruits start ripening in August.

Bearberry is also known as *kinnikinnick*, an Algonquin word that means "smoking mixture" and alludes to Native American tribes using the dried leaves in pipes. It also has a long history of use as a medicinal plant that is believed to protect the immune system, alleviate headaches, reduce

inflammation, and prevent urinary tract infections. Bearberry might induce labor and should not be used during pregnancy; in large doses, it can also cause symptoms such as nausea, vomiting, fever, and chills.

The fruits lack flavor, but the leaves, which have a strong, earthy flavor, can be used fresh or dried in tea. It's often called uva ursi tea.

In Your Glass:

Add 2 teaspoons (10ml) of dried bearberry leaves to 2 cups (480ml) of boiling water; steep for at least fifteen minutes. Strain the leaves before sipping. To make iced tea, steep 2 teaspoons (10ml) of dried bearberry leaves in 2 cups (480ml) of boiling water; steep overnight. Strain the leaves and pour over ice.

BEE BALM
(*Monarda fistulosa*)
■ ZONES: 3 TO 9

Bee balm, also known as wild bergamot, is popular in pollinator gardens because pollinators such as bees and butterflies like the nectar-rich flowers. The fragrant perennial herb, a member of the mint family, produces clusters of pom-pom-like flowers atop square stems. Bee balm blooms from July to September.

The Oswego Indians used bee balm in teas, so the earliest versions of the herbal teas were called Oswego tea. Different kinds of bee balm have different flavors. The leaves of scarlet bee balm (*Monarda didyma*) have a light citrus flavor; lavender bee balm has a stronger flavor that is most similar to bergamot orange. Although bee balm smells like Earl Grey tea and was even used as a replacement for black tea after the Boston Tea Party, the essential oil used in the iconic tea is from a different plant. The leaves of bee balm make amazing citrus-flavored tea and can be used fresh or dried.

Bee balm grows well in sun to part shade and well-drained soil. Like other mints, bee balm can be aggressive. In the garden, divide the plant in the fall to keep growth in check or plant it in containers to keep it from taking over—but be sure that the containers are large enough. Bee balm starts out small but grows to 2 to 4 feet (60cm to 1.2m) tall and can spread up to 3 feet (90cm). The plant is prone to powdery mildew; any leaves that show the telltale signs—circular white spots on the leaves, yellowing, and wilting—should not be used in tea.

The herb is a natural source of thymol, an antiseptic used in mouthwash. Oil from the leaves has been used for a range of ailments from respiratory infections and fevers to stomachaches, headaches, and insomnia.

In Your Glass:

Using bee balm to make tea is a natural choice, or add the citrus-flavored herb to a mojito. You can also mix 2 tablespoons (10ml) of fresh bee balm leaves with ½ cup (120ml) of club soda, 1½ ounces (45ml) of white rum, 1 tablespoon (15ml) of honey, and 1 tablespoon (15ml) of lemon juice for a refreshing bee-themed cocktail.

CARDAMOM
(*Elettaria cardamomum*)

■ ZONES: 10 TO 13

Cardamom, often called Queen of Spices, is one of the most expensive spices in the world. The tropical plant is labor intensive to grow; the small seed pods used to produce

the prized spice are slow to ripen and can take years to mature. After harvesting, the pods must be washed and dried. Green cardamom (so-called for the color of the pods) is harvested before the pods mature and has a sweeter flavor; black cardamom is dried and has its seeds extracted, resulting in a more pungent flavor. Cardamom gives chai its distinctive flavor.

Cardamom is native to tropical and subtropical climates like India, Sri Lanka, and Indonesia. In most of North America (zones 9 and lower), cardamom must be grown indoors or in greenhouses. The plants, which can grow up to 10 feet (3.1m) tall, do not tolerate drought. Choose a location with a lot of filtered sunlight and a lot of space to spread out.

Cineole, one of the essential oils in cardamom, is a potent antiseptic hailed for killing bacteria and banishing bad breath, making the pods popular breath fresheners. Research has also found that cardamom improves glucose intolerance, reduces inflammation, and helps prevent weight gain.

In Your Glass:

Cardamom tea is a popular hot beverage in parts of Asia. To make tea, add 1 teaspoon (5ml) of ground cardamom to 2 cups (480ml) of hot (not boiling) water and steep for five minutes. Strain the cardamom before drinking. Cardamom pairs well with other strong flavors, including cloves and cinnamon.

CATNIP
(*Nepeta cataria*)
■ **ZONES:** 3 TO 7

Cats go wild for this intoxicating herb. Although it gives felines a natural high, the perennial is known for its calming effect in humans.

Catnip contains nepetalactone, the active ingredient in the herbal sedative valerian, so it's used to tame anxiety, insomnia, and nervousness, and it boosts mood. Its sedative effects can cause drowsiness, so drink beverages with catnip in the evening, not first thing in the morning, and avoid drinking catnip tea and driving. Catnip is also effective for indigestion, stomach cramps, and gas. The herb might stimulate uterine contractions and trigger menstruation, so pregnant women and those with menstrual disorders, such as pelvic inflammatory disease, should not use catnip.

The perennial is native to Europe and parts of Asia but has adapted well to the United States. It grows up to 3 feet (90cm) tall and just as wide. In cooler climates, you can plant catnip in full sun, but opt for part shade in areas where it's hot and humid because those conditions can cause its demise. Catnip is drought tolerant and prefers drier soils.

Pollinators are drawn to the flowers, which are white with pale purple markings and bloom from spring through fall. After the flowers bloom, snip the flower spikes to encourage a second bloom period. Plant catnip in containers because this member of the mint family is a vigorous spreader.

The fragrant gray-green leaves have a mild mint flavor with a hint of citrus (adding a lemony herb like lemon verbena or lemon balm enhances the citrus flavor). Catnip can be used fresh or dried.

Catmint (*Nepeta mussinii*) can also be used for tea. The plants are similar, but catmint, with its showier purple flowers, is more ornamental than catnip; different kinds of catmint have less aggressive growth habits.

 *In Your Glass:*

Use catnip in hot tea or add 1 tablespoon (15ml) of dried catnip per 5 ounces (150ml) of brandy (to make an infused brandy) and shake vigorously, then let it steep for at least thirty minutes; strain the catnip and add the infused spirit to violet simple syrup, cream, and brandy to make a milky cocktail.

CHICKWEED

(*Cerastium arvense*)

■ **ZONES:** 3 TO 8

This plant thrives in open spaces such as lawns and pastures, leading it to be considered more of a noxious weed than a flavorful herb. The perennial spreads via rhizomes and taproots, which cause it to form dense mats that can spread up to 3 feet (90cm) wide. Delicate white flowers bloom from April to August.

Multiple kinds of chickweed can be found worldwide. Field chickweed (*C. arvense*) is native to North America. Common chickweed (*Stellaria media*) and mouse-ear chickweed (*C. fontanum*) are native to Europe and now grow across the United States. All species have earned a reputation as weeds and are often killed with herbicides.

Most chickweed prefers cooler climates and often pops up in alpine areas, thriving beneath tree canopies. In areas where summer temperatures are sweltering, chickweed struggles to survive. The herb grows best in full sun and drier soils; too much moisture can cause root rot.

 *In Your Glass:*

Chickweed makes delicious tea. Add 2 tablespoons (30ml) of fresh chickweed or 1 tablespoon (15ml) of dried chickweed to 1 cup (240ml) of boiling water and steep for at least five minutes. Strain the greens before drinking. It can also be used as a garnish.

Harvest chickweed to appreciate its fresh flavor, which is often compared to that of corn silks. Chickweed contains beta-carotene, calcium, magnesium, potassium, selenium, and vitamin C. It's used for digestion, constipation, asthma, inflammation, and muscle and joint pain. The leaves, stems, flowers, and seeds can all be eaten raw or cooked.

CHOCOLATE MINT
(*Mentha × piperita 'Chocolate'*)

■ **ZONES:** 5 TO 9

Despite its name, this perennial herb doesn't taste like chocolate. Instead, chocolate mint has a strong peppermint flavor similar to the mint flavor in peppermint patties—though some people claim that it's possible to detect subtle chocolate notes.

Chocolate mint is a cultivar of peppermint. Although the perennial herb, like other kinds of mint, is good for

it to grow 2 feet (60cm) tall and 2 feet (60cm) wide.

You can start new plants from cuttings. Grow chocolate mint in containers to keep it from taking over the garden, and move the containers indoors to overwinter in a sunny window. Chocolate mint prefers full sun but will tolerate part shade; keep soil moist and harvest the leaves before the plant flowers.

headaches, digestion, and fevers, its real benefit is its culinary uses. The dark green to purplish leaves are great on their own, fresh or dried, in a cup of mint tea. The cool menthol flavor is also excellent in hot chocolate and baked goods.

Like all herbs in the mint family, chocolate mint spreads rapidly. Pinching back the leaves will keep it from going to seed, and regular division can prevent its aggressive spread. Although chocolate mint is smaller than other mints, expect

 *In Your Glass:*

Chocolate mint has myriad uses in drinks, from peppermint martinis and mojitos to tea. Adding 1 tablespoon (15ml) of fresh chocolate mint to black tea gives it a hint of peppermint; the cool menthol flavor is also excellent in hot chocolate.

CILANTRO/CORIANDER

(Coriandrum sativum)

■ **ZONES:** 2 TO 11

Cilantro, typically called coriander in the United Kingdom, might seem like an odd addition to a beverage garden, but the annual herb has a complex flavor that's been described as fresh and citrus-like (though some people have a genetic trait that makes it taste like soap to them). It's a unique plant that produces two distinct spices: the leaves are sold as cilantro, and the seeds, which ripen in small, round pods, are sold as coriander. The leaves on the bottom of the plant are broader and more parsley-like, while the newer leaves at the top of the plant are more delicate. Mature seeds also have a hint of citrus and, when roasted, a nuttier flavor.

Cilantro produces seasonal flowers in white, pink, and pale purple, and it grows up to 2 feet (60cm) tall. It's considered a cool-weather annual. In hot climates, cilantro is known to bolt, a process that leads plants to go to seed and die. To keep cilantro from bolting, either pinch off the flowers or plant in late summer, after the hottest part of the season, and harvest in fall.

Cilantro grows well in gardens or containers. For the herb to thrive, plant it in well-drained soil and part shade. Beware of planting in full sun; if the heat is too intense, cilantro could succumb to sunscald.

Both the leaves and the seeds of this herb are chock full of nutrients. Cilantro (the leaves) contains vitamins A and K, folate, potassium, manganese, and beta-carotene; coriander (the seeds) has several minerals, including calcium, magnesium, and potassium. The herb is believed to combat bacterial infections, ease digestive upset, lower blood sugar, improve sleep, and protect against colon cancer.

 *In Your Glass:*

The flavor of cilantro, best described as a mild combination of mint and citrus, complements watermelon, lime, bananas, and grapefruit in cocktails, infused water, and smoothies. Mix ¼ cup (60ml) of fresh cilantro leaves with 2 ounces (60ml) of tequila, 1½ ounces (45ml) of fresh lime juice, and 1 ounce (30ml) of simple syrup (recipe on page 124) to make a cilantro margarita.

EUCALYPTUS
(*Eucalyptus perriniana*)
■ **ZONES:** 8 TO 10

Ubiquitous in Australia, eucalyptus is less common in the United States because it requires tropical growing conditions, including full sun and fertile, well-drained soil. Regular pruning is required for the broadleaf evergreen to maintain its bushy appearance. In colder climates, you can grow eucalyptus indoors, provided you place it in a south-facing window and keep the soil moist. However, the fast-growing plant, which can reach 30 feet (9.1m) in height, is apt to outgrow its pot too quickly to make it a popular houseplant. A cold snap can kill eucalyptus.

Despite the challenges of growing eucalyptus, the health benefits associated with the tropical plant make it a worthwhile endeavor. The oil from the gray-green leaves of the eucalyptus tree has antimicrobial and antibacterial properties that can help ease colds, sore throats, bronchitis, and respiratory problems. Research has also found eucalyptus to be an effective pain reliever, easing pain associated with joint strains, arthritis, and backaches.

 *In Your Glass:*

Eucalyptus tea is made from adding 1 tablespoon (15 ml) of crushed, fresh eucalyptus leaves to 2 cups (480 ml) of boiling water and letting it steep for up to ten minutes; strain the leaves before drinking. Thanks to the sweet menthol flavor, eucalyptus has a cooling sensation, though the flavor is often described as bitter. Crushing the leaves helps release the flavor. Ginger is a good flavor complement.

FENNEL

(*Foeniculum vulgare*)

■ **ZONES:** 4 TO 9

In the Middle Ages, hanging fennel over doors was believed to keep out evil spirits. Today, the herb is prized for its medicinal uses. Fennel is used for digestion, gastrointestinal distress, appetite regulation, metabolism, hypertension, congestion, and menstrual cramps. The herb is antibacterial, antifungal, and anti-inflammatory.

You can grow fennel as a perennial herb or an annual bulb. As an herb, fennel is a perennial that produces green foliage and seeds used in herbal medicine. The bulb (*F. vulgare* var. *azoricum*) is also known as anise fennel because of its amazing licorice flavor. You can plant bulbs in spring and fall, providing two annual harvests.

The bulbous base, thick stocks, and feathered fronds make fennel look like a cross between two of its relatives: celery and dill. Clusters of small yellow flowers appear on the ends of short stalks, creating the appearance of a flat flower head. The bloom period ends in July, and seeds replace the flowers. Harvest just as the flowers start to fade. Clip the stems with the flower heads and hang them in a dark spot until dried.

Grow fennel in full sun and moist soil, where it will grow up to 6 feet (1.8m) tall and 3 feet (90cm) wide. To keep fennel from self-seeding and taking over the garden, remove the flowering stems before seeds appear.

Fennel is a larval plant for certain swallowtail butterflies; bees also love the flowers. The licorice flavor makes fennel popular as a culinary herb that is eaten raw, dried, stewed, or grilled. When making tea, adding fennel seeds to boiling water can destroy the nutrients.

 *In Your Glass:*

Make fennel simple syrup from 1 tablespoon (15ml) of fennel seeds, 1 cup (240ml) of sugar, and 1 cup (240ml) of water; add it to 2 cups (480ml) of sparkling water, add 2 tablespoons (30ml) of honey, and garnish with cucumber to make a fennel spritzer. Fennel can also be added to cocktails, including martinis, and mocktails. In juices, smoothies, and tea, combine fennel with citrus or mint to help balance its strong anise flavor.

HOLY BASIL
(*Ocimum sanctum*)
■ ZONES: 2 TO 11

The significance of this "holy" herb is as impressive as its flavor. Holy basil was said to be growing around Christ's tomb after the resurrection, and, in some Greek Orthodox churches, it's used to prepare holy water. In India, the tender perennial is called *tulsi*, which means "the incomparable one."

Different varieties of holy basil have different flavors. Rama is the most common and has lighter green leaves and a stronger, more clove-like taste; Vana, which often grows wild, is the most fragrant and has notes of licorice; and Krishna, with its dark green, almost purple, leaves, has a stronger, peppery flavor. All varieties of tulsi are more aromatic and sweeter than traditional Italian basil and can be a sweet complement to tart flavors like ginger, cinnamon, and turmeric. It's known for alleviating digestive upset, relieving stress, and calming colds.

Holy basil, native to Africa and Asia, grows best in hot temperatures and drier soil (if basil is watered too often, it will rot).

It blooms from June to first frost. Although the herb is sensitive to frost, it's possible to place root cuttings in water and overwinter the rooted plants in a sunny window. The flavor is at its peak when the leaves just start to bud, but leaves can also be dried and used in a variety of beverages. Lemon basil (*Ocimum × citriodorum* or *Ocimum × africanum*) is a lemon-scented basil with a light citrus flavor. The plant has lime green and white variegated leaves that can be dried or used fresh; lemon basil also has a heady scent that makes it a popular garnish.

In Your Glass:

This versatile herb is often added to iced tea, lemonade, water, tea, and cocktails. The pairings you choose will depend on the type of holy basil you choose. The licorice flavor of Vana is delicious alongside citrus, mint, and lavender. Use it to make infused water by adding ¼ cup (60ml) of chopped, fresh holy basil leaves to 2 cups (480ml) of boiling water. Let it steep for fifteen minutes, strain the herbs, let the water cool, refrigerate overnight, and serve over ice for a refreshing, slightly sweet drink.

LAVENDER MINT

(*Mentha* × *piperita* 'Lavender')

■ **ZONES:** 5 TO 9

Lavender mint, as its name suggests, has a rich lavender flavor and floral scent. The leaves have light purple undersides, and the flowers, which bloom from June to September, are both lavender in color and scent.

Like all mints, lavender mint is fast growing, prefers full sun to part shade, and likes moist, well-drained soil. It grows up to 2 feet (60cm) tall and spreads 2 feet (60cm) (or more) wide. It's a red-stemmed mint (like peppermint) and is often used dried, but fresh lavender mint can be used in beverages, too.

In Your Glass:

The sweet flavor is the perfect addition to lemonade, iced tea, and floral cocktails and mocktails. Add lavender mint simple syrup (add 1 tablespoon [15ml] of chopped, fresh lavender mint leaves to the simple syrup recipe on page 124) to one bottle of prosecco; add lavender mint leaves to garnish. Lavender mint can be combined with lavender for tea that is floral in both flavor and fragrance; lemon herbs also complement the flavor.

LEMON BALM

(*Melissa officinalis*)

■ **ZONES:** 3 TO 7

The name is a little misleading. While this perennial herb has a lemon scent and citrus flavor, lemon balm is actually a member of the mint family. The flavor is best described as light, and recipes featuring lemon balm as an ingredient often call for lemon juice, too, because the herb is mild.

Lemon balm spreads like other mint species, making it best confined to a container where it won't take over the garden. The low-growing herb grows about 18 inches (45cm) high and is often used as ground cover. Bees love the white and yellow flowers that bloom from June to August; in fact, the herb was once called bee balm. Plant it in full sun and water it often; regular pruning during the growing season helps keep it from going to seed or spreading too fast.

As a medicinal herb, lemon balm is used to reduce stress and anxiety and promote sleep. It loses much of its flavor after it's dried, so lemon balm is best brewed fresh. Be careful not to bruise the leaves during harvesting; to dry, hang the cuttings in a moisture-free environment so the stems don't rot.

 *In Your Glass:*

Lemon balm works well in lemonade, of course, but plan to add lemon juice, too, because lemon balm is too mild to pack much of a citrus punch. To make lemonade, add ½ cup (120ml) of fresh lemon balm leaves (crushed) and some sugar to 3 cups (720ml) of boiling water; stir until the sugar dissolves, and let it steep for fifteen minutes. Add juice from four lemons, refrigerate overnight, and serve over ice. Even with a handful of fresh leaves, drinks made with lemon balm tea will only have a mild, minty flavor

LEMONGRASS

(*Cymbopogon citratus*)

■ **ZONES:** 8 TO 11

A tender perennial that looks like clumps of tall grass, lemongrass is best known as a fragrant addition to Asian dishes. It's native to India and Sri Lanka and prized around the globe for its health benefits, which range from easing sore throats and reducing inflammation to aiding in digestion and alleviating headaches.

Lemongrass grows wild in tropical grasslands. In warmer climates in the United States, the clumping grass requires more attention. Lemongrass, an evergreen in zones 10 and higher, grows up to 4 feet

(1.2m) tall and 3 feet (90cm) wide and performs best in full sun. You can also plant it in containers and grow it indoors.

For the best flavor, harvest lemongrass when the stalks are firm, green on the top, and light yellow on the bottom; avoid leaves with brown edges. Store fresh lemongrass in the refrigerator or freezer or cut it into pieces and dry it.

Lemongrass has bright green foliage with a powerful scent that makes it a common ingredient in perfume and soap. The flavor is strong, too. As its name suggests, lemongrass has a zesty citrus flavor; you can use it fresh or dried without sacrificing flavor.

The leaves are sharp and inedible. You must mash the grass with a mortar and pestle or put it through a food grinder; even then, the blades can still be sharp, so it's essential to strain drinks well to avoid swallowing any pieces of the plant.

 *In Your Glass:*

Add lemongrass to lemonade, tea, or soda. Making lemongrass soda is as simple as adding 3 stalks of chopped lemongrass to 2 cups (480ml) of club soda and 1 cup (240ml) of sugar; bring the ingredients to a boil, reduce heat and simmer for ten minutes, strain the lemongrass, let cool, and serve over ice. The citrus flavor pairs well with mint, cucumber, bay leaves, and ginger. Lemongrass is also a popular ingredient in cocktails and mocktails such as gin and tonics, mojitos, martinis, or mint juleps.

LEMON VERBENA
(*Aloysia citriodora*)
■ **ZONES:** 8 TO 10

This deciduous shrub, also known as lemon beebrush, lemon luisa, and Hierba Luisa, is native to South America. Lemon verbena can grow up to 15 feet (4.6m) tall.

The narrow leaves grow in groups of three around the stems, and clusters of small white to lavender flowers bloom in the summer and fall.

The leaves have such a powerful citrus scent that lemon verbena is often considered the strongest of the lemon-scented plants. Lemon verbena wasn't just named for its scent; the lemon flavor is intense, too. In fact, the leaves are often used as a substitute for lemon zest in recipes. Both the leaves and flowers, fresh or dried, are used in teas. The flavor is best when the leaves are fresh; dried lemon verbena has a milder flavor, but, even when it's subtle, the lemon is unmistakable. The flavor in the leaves is strongest during flowering. It only takes a small number of leaves to brew a strong cup of lemon tea.

Lemon verbena is said to be good for relieving heartburn and indigestion; it's also said to be a sedative that helps alleviate insomnia and anxiety.

Plant lemon verbena in light shade and moist, well-drained soil, and prune the leaves throughout the growing season to maintain its shape. This low-maintenance herb can be overwintered indoors in a bright but cool spot.

In Your Glass:

Take advantage of the strong citrus flavor to make gimlets, gin and tonics, or other bright, citrus cocktails. Lemon verbena can also be used in a simple syrup: follow the recipe for basic simple syrup on page 124 and add 1 cup (240ml) of packed lemon verbena leaves. To cut the lemon flavor in any recipe, add strawberries, mint, or vanilla. Together with mint, it makes an excellent herbal tea.

MARJORAM
(*Origanum majorana*)

■ **ZONES:** 9 TO 10

A relative of oregano, this Mediterranean herb has a milder, more delicate flavor. It's grown as a tender perennial in warmer climates; further north, marjoram grows well as an annual.

The aromatic and flavorful gray-green leaves make marjoram a popular culinary herb that is often used in stews, roasts, and stuffing; the leaves can also be steeped to make tea. As a medicinal herb, marjoram is believed to be beneficial for treating cold and flu symptoms such as runny nose, cough, and infection. It is also used for digestive issues, migraines, and nerve pain, though studies on its effectiveness are limited. Small studies have shown that marjoram improves cardiovascular health by reducing blood pressure and improving blood flow.

Marjoram prefers full sun and neutral or alkaline soils with a lot of sandy loam; a low-maintenance plant, it tolerates heat and drought. The low-growing plants can get up to 2 feet (60cm) tall and produce white to pale pink flowers during the summer months. Harvest marjoram before it flowers, when the flavor of the leaves is at its peak. Cutting the stems before the plant flowers will also make the plant bushier. Use marjoram leaves fresh or dried.

 *In Your Glass:*

Marjoram makes excellent tea. Mix 1 teaspoon (5ml) of fresh marjoram leaves or ½ teaspoon (2.5ml) of dried marjoram with 1 cup (240ml) of boiling water and let the tea steep for three to five minutes. Strain the leaves before serving.

PARSLEY
(*Petroselinum crispum*)
■ **ZONES:** 2 TO 11

Parsley has been relegated to the side of the plate for too long. Though it's most commonly used as a garnish, parsley is both delicious and nutritious. The Mediterranean herb is high in vitamins A and C and minerals like potassium, iron, and copper. It has been used to prevent kidney stones, relieve joint pain, and combat anemia;

parsley has also been declared an anticancer powerhouse, thanks to studies that show it combats free radicals, prevents cell damage that can lead to cancer, and inhibits tumor growth. Parsley is known to increase menstrual flow and should not be used by pregnant women.

This annual grows in full sun to part shade and moist, well-drained soil. It prefers cooler climates and can wilt in hot, humid summers. Avoid growing parsley from seed because it has a long germination period. It's possible to overwinter herbs indoors in a bright window.

Parsley has a light, fresh flavor with a hint of bitterness. Curly parsley (var. *crispum*) and Italian parsley (var. *neapolitanum*) are among the most common varieties of the popular herb. Although Italian parsley has a stronger flavor, the varieties can be used interchangeably.

 *In Your Glass:*

While parsley makes a great garnish, it can also be used both fresh and dried as an ingredient in a range of beverages. Add the leafy herb to infused waters, smoothies, iced tea, cocktails, and mocktails. You can also steep 2 tablespoons (30ml) of fresh parsley leaves in 1 cup (240ml) of boiling water to make tea. Steep for two or three minutes, strain the leaves, and sip. Parsley loses its flavor when it's exposed to heat, so keep the steep time to a minimum. Parsley is compatible with mint, rosemary, thyme, basil, and berries.

PEPPERMINT
(*Mentha × piperita*)
■ ZONES: 5 TO 9

Peppermint might be mistaken as a species all its own, but it was developed by crossing watermint (*Mentha aquatica*) and spearmint (*Mentha spicata*). The result is an herbaceous perennial with robust mint flavor and fragrance. The leaves from fresh peppermint plants have a stronger flavor than dried leaves, but both are strong enough to make delicious drinks.

The hybrid mint isn't just a popular herbal tea ingredient; peppermint is also known as a powerful medicinal herb that is used to soothe upset stomachs and aid in digestion; its numbing effect also makes it effective for treating headaches, depression, and anxiety.

Peppermint grows in full sun to part shade and tolerates high temperatures as long as it's watered often and the soil is kept moist. Since it's a hybrid, peppermint is sterile and cannot be grown from seed; root it from cuttings instead.

 *In Your Glass:*

It is hard to find a drink that doesn't benefit from the addition of peppermint. Add the minty herb to tea, lemonade, and infused water. Peppermint is also a great choice for cocktails and mocktails made with chocolate, cinnamon, lime, strawberries, or vanilla. It is an essential ingredient in a mint julep (see the recipe on page 132).

Pretty pink flowers bloom in July and August—remove them after bloom to stimulate new growth. The plant, which grows up to 2 feet (60cm) high and 2 feet (60cm) wide, grows aggressively. Peppermint's rapid spread has earned it a spot on the USDA's invasive species list. Plant it in containers to keep it from taking over the garden.

PINEAPPLE SAGE

(*Salvia elegans*)

■ **ZONES:** 8 TO 11

Hummingbirds and butterflies love pineapple sage's pretty tubular, scarlet flowers, which bloom between August and October, while tipplers appreciate the citrus flavor and scent that earned it its moniker.

The tender perennial is native to Mexico and Central America, where it grows as a small, clumping shrub that reaches up to 4 feet (1.2m) high and 3 feet (90cm) wide.

In zones 7 and lower, you can grow pineapple sage as an annual that will survive until the first frost; alternatively, you can grow it in pots and overwinter it indoors. Pineapple sage grows best in full sun and well-drained soil.

Despite its name, pineapple sage has no relation to the pineapple plant or the sage plant. It's a member of the same Lamiaceae family as mint. Like other mints, it eases upset stomachs and aids in digestion; pineapple sage might be calming (some studies show it has mild antidepressant effects), and it is often used to treat sleep disorders.

Pineapple sage is a mild herb. Crush the leaves to release the fragrance and tangy citrus flavor. The red flowers are edible, too, and taste like citrus and mint. Use fresh or dried leaves and flowers in your favorite drinks.

 *In Your Glass:*

Use pineapple sage to make simple syrup (see the recipe for mint simple syrup on page 125) that can be used (with muddled mint) in pineapple sage mojitos. It also tastes great in hot and iced teas.

ROSEMARY

(*Rosmarinus officinalis*)

■ **ZONES:** 8 TO 10

One of the most popular culinary herbs, rosemary is native to the Mediterranean and often paired with heartier fare, such as lamb, pork, and potatoes. It's prized for the strong aroma of its thin, needle-like gray-green leaves and its robust flavor, which is best described as minty with light pine notes—not surprising, given that it's a woody herb.

Rosemary is hailed as a natural health powerhouse that aids in digestion, enhances cognitive function, reduces inflammation, and improves liver function. It is also known to cause side effects, ranging from nausea and vomiting to uterine contractions— pregnant women should avoid it.

Grow this perennial shrub in full sun and acidic soil. In colder climates, you can overwinter rosemary indoors, provided it receives enough sunlight (or artificial light). Don't overwater rosemary; it prefers drier soil. If it's overwatered, the plants will develop root rot. Pruning plants after the white flowers bloom in June or July helps encourage denser foliage growth. If left to grow wild, rosemary will get lanky.

Rather than stripping the leaves from the stems to make drinks, use the entire sprig to achieve the best flavor. Young stems have the strongest flavor, but older stems (and dried rosemary) also produce great-tasting tea. You can also turn rosemary into a powder. To do this, remove the leaves from the stem and then place ¼ cup (60ml) of rosemary in the microwave for two to three minutes (or until the leaves start to crumble when touched). Use a mortar and pestle to crumble the leaves into a powder.

 *In Your Glass:*

A sprig of rosemary is a popular garnish, but it can also be used in cocktails from creative to classic. In an old fashioned, rosemary simple syrup adds an herbaceous note when combined with rye whiskey and orange bitters. Make a rosemary gimlet with rosemary simple syrup (follow the mint simple syrup recipe on page 125, substituting mint with rosemary) and add 1 ounce (30ml) to 2 ounces (60ml) of gin and ½ ounce (15ml) of lime juice.

SAGE

(*Salvia officinalis*)

■ **ZONES:** 4 TO 8

Though sage grows well in cooler climates, the herb is native to the Mediterranean and northern Africa, where it has a long record of medicinal use. Native Americans also used sage in their healing rituals. Research shows that sage can be effective for easing sore throats, lowering cholesterol,

improving mood, and protecting against neurological disorders, such as dementia. Thanks to a compound called thujone found in some of the 900-plus kinds of sage, too much of the herb might cause

restlessness, vomiting, rapid heart rate, vertigo, or seizures.

The easy-to-grow perennial herb produces oblong gray-green leaves on woody stems. It grows like a small shrub, reaching 2½ feet (75cm) tall and wide. In June, sage blooms with light purple to blue flowers. The tubular blooms, which can reach up to 1 inch (2.5cm) in length, grow on upright stalks, and their nectar attracts bees and butterflies. Grow sage in full sun and let the soil dry out between watering. If the soil is too wet, sage can succumb to root rot.

Sage has fragrant leaves and an astringent flavor that has been described as a cross between citrus and eucalyptus; it's sweet with a hint of bitterness; and it can be used fresh or dried.

In Your Glass:

Sage is great in cocktails. Use the herb to make a simple syrup (follow the mint simple syrup recipe on page 125, substituting mint for sage) or add fresh leaves to cocktails made with gin, bourbon, or tequila. Sage complements other herbs, such as rosemary and thyme, but also works well with pineapple, grapefruit, and other citrus flavors.

SPEARMINT

(*Mentha spicata*)

■ **ZONES:** 5 TO 9

Spearmint is one of the more delicate mints. Its sweet flavor is a natural complement to other sweet ingredients, including lavender and chamomile, but the herb also works well with savory spices such as cinnamon and winter savory (*Satureja hortensis*), another member of the mint family.

The perennial ground cover prefers sun or part shade and medium to wet soil. It grows up to 2 feet (60cm) tall and 2 feet (60cm) wide and produces delicate white, light pink, or lavender flowers that attract butterflies during their summertime bloom. Each type of spearmint has large, toothed leaves, but 'Kentucky Colonel' mint—the cultivar preferred for mint juleps and mojitos—has larger (and arguably more attractive) leaves.

Clip spearmint after it blooms to promote growth. The herb grows rapidly, so you will need to divide it seasonally; plant it in pots to

keep it from spreading where it's not wanted. While you can harvest spearmint throughout the season, the leaves become bitter after the plant flowers, so for the best flavors, harvest before blooms appear. The flavors are best when leaves are fresh, not dried.

Spearmint has been shown to manage inflammation, boost the immune system, and alleviate digestive upset. It's not recommended for pregnant women because it could damage the uterus; excessive consumption could also cause kidney damage.

 *In Your Glass:*

Spearmint, like other mints, is a popular addition to a range of beverages, from tea and water to cocktails and smoothies. To make infused water, add ½ cup (120ml) of fresh spearmint leaves and two limes, sliced, to 2 quarts (1.9 liters) of water; mix together and refrigerate overnight.

STINGING NETTLE
(*Urtica dioica*)

■ ZONES: 3 TO 10

Stinging nettle is a staple in herbal medicine. Its leaves are excellent sources of vitamins A, C, and K; several B vitamins; beta-carotene; calcium; copper; iron; magnesium; and potassium. The perennial herb is used for allergies, muscle aches, urinary tract infections, and inflammatory diseases

such as osteoarthritis and gout. However, it can stimulate uterine contractions and shouldn't be used when pregnant. Despite its nutritional value and healing properties, stinging nettle isn't a popular garden plant. The herb is often used as a stand-in for spinach because it has a bitter flavor.

The fast-growing plant is often considered an aggressive weed. It grows wild under forest canopies, alongside streams, and in pastures, where it thrives because the stems and undersides of the leaves are covered in small hairs (trichomes) that wildlife avoid. The trichomes release histamine-based fluids when broken. (The genus name *Urtica*

comes from a Latin word that means "to burn," and it was so named for the burning sensation it causes when the trichomes penetrate the skin.)

Stinging nettle prefers full sun and damp, rich soil. In ideal conditions, stinging nettle can grow up to 4 feet (1.2m) tall. A distant cousin to mint, stinging nettle is also fast spreading and, if left unchecked, will take over the garden. Grow it in containers and prune often, or harvest in the wild (in areas not sprayed with pesticides).

The small hairs are sharp, so it's best to wear gloves, long pants, and long sleeves when planting and harvesting stinging nettle. Choose a spot in the garden that pets and children cannot access to prevent them from coming in contact with the prickly plants.

 *In Your Glass:*

Stinging nettle can be used to make tea. Add 2 tablespoons (30ml) of dried nettle leaves to 4 cups (960ml) of water; steep for thirty minutes and strain the leaves before drinking. It has a bitter flavor (making it a popular stand-in for spinach). If you use it in smoothies, add yogurt to tone down the bitterness.

ST. JOHN'S WORT
(*Hypericum calycinum*)
■ **ZONES:** 5 TO 9

This popular medicinal herb is perhaps best known as a natural antidepressant. Researchers believe that hypericin, a natural chemical compound in the plant, helps improve mood by acting on neurotransmitters in the brain. St. John's wort also contains hyperforin, a powerful reuptake inhibitor of brain chemicals such as serotonin and dopamine that play a role in depression. It's believed to be as effective in treating mild to moderate depression as prescription medication.

In addition to its mood-boosting benefits, St. John's wort is also used to treat wounds and alleviate hot flashes during menopause. It's such a potent medicinal herb that France has banned products made with St. John's wort because of potential interactions with some medications. There are also concerns that it might contribute to dementia in those diagnosed with Alzheimer's disease, worsen symptoms of attention deficit/hyperactivity disorder, trigger mania in those with bipolar disorder or psychosis in those with schizophrenia, and impair fertility. For these reasons, use this herb with great caution.

St. John's wort is an easy-to-grow deciduous shrub native to southern Europe and Asia. Grow it as a ground cover—its maximum height is 18 inches (45cm)—in full sun to part shade. It prefers well-drained, sandy soil. Root rot is common in hot, humid climates.

Large yellow flowers that resemble roses bloom in July and August. Cut back leaves in late winter or early spring to promote vigorous new growth. St. John's wort grows rapidly, spreading via underground stems, and is considered an invasive plant in some areas of the United States because it chokes out native plants. Keep growth in check by planting the herb in containers. The herb is also toxic to livestock and shouldn't be planted in or around pastures.

In Your Glass:

This medicinal herb is most commonly used in tea; both the leaves and flowers can be used. Steep 3 teaspoons (15ml) of fresh leaves or flowers in 1 cup (240ml) of boiling water for four minutes; strain the herb before drinking. The flowers have a light lemon flavor; the leaves are earthier and more pungent. **Do not use St. John's wort in cocktails**, as it interacts with the alcohol and may cause symptoms like dizziness and drowsiness.

TEA PLANT
(*Camellia sinensis*)
■ ZONES: 7 TO 9

All types of tea—white, green, black, and oolong—come from one plant: *Camellia sinensis*.

Although the leaves and buds of all varieties of *Camellia sinensis* can be used to make tea, *C. sinensis* var. *sinensis* is the most common. Native to China, the plant has smaller leaves and favors drier, cooler climates, making it ideal for higher elevations.

The evergreen shrubs have been cultivated for thousands of years; the tea plant is so ubiquitous in its native Southeast Asia that plants have been found growing wild across the continent. In the United States, tea can be grown in zones 7 to 9 and, in cooler climates, overwintered in greenhouses or high tunnels (which are plastic-covered tunnels similar to greenhouses). It's also possible to grow tea plants in pots; use a camellia/azalea soil mix.

Plant *Camellia sinensis* in spring or fall. The tea plant grows up to 15 feet (4.6m) tall and 10 feet (3m) wide and produces white flowers between October and December. It prefers part shade; choose a location where plants are protected from strong winds. It grows best in acidic soil with a pH of 6.5 or lower. Control the size and shape by pruning branches after flowering.

Growing tea requires patience. It takes about three years before tea leaves can be harvested. Once the plants reach maturity, pick young shoots with two to three leaves and use them to make white, green, black, or oolong tea. Different processing creates the different types of tea. The following pages will explain how to harvest and process each type.

WHITE TEA

White tea is the least processed type of tea. Made with the soft, unopened leaf bud on the tip of each stem, white tea—named for the white color of the buds—is the sweetest and mildest tea. Harvest in early spring when the buds are still closed.

Wither: Spread the buds out on a tray in a warm, humid area with good circulation and leave them out for a few hours. This process is called withering because the leaves dry out and start to look and feel withered.

Dry: Put the buds in the oven at 120°F (50°C) for twenty minutes, shifting them several times. You can also dry the buds in a food dehydrator, but the higher temperatures can have a negative impact on the flavor.

Sip: Add 1 teaspoon (5ml) of buds to hot—but not boiling—water and let steep for two to three minutes. Strain the buds before sipping.

GREEN TEA

Green tea is made from the tender, light green leaves that appear in the spring. Though green tea is not a highly processed form of tea, it still undergoes a specific process between plant and cup. Harvest the top two leaves and the leaf bud from the plant and follow these steps.

Steam: Insert a steamer into a saucepan filled with ½ inch (1.5cm) of water, cover, and let it boil. Once the water reaches a rolling boil, add the leaves and cover again, steaming the leaves for two minutes. This stops the leaves from oxidizing and releases the fresh, just-picked flavor in the leaves.

Cool: Remove the pan and run the leaves under cold water.

Roll: Roll the leaves between your palms to shape them. There is no correct shape; turn them into small balls or tubes. The goal is to make tight shapes so that it's easier to dry the leaves. Working the leaves into tight balls or tubes releases the moisture, turning the leaves brown.

Dry: Spread the rolled leaves on a baking dish and put them into a preheated oven at 230°F (110°C) for ten minutes. The leaves should become dry and brittle.

Sip: Add 1 teaspoon (5ml) of buds to a cup of boiling water and let steep for three to five minutes. Strain the buds before sipping.

Green tea leaves can be used immediately after undergoing the drying process or stored in an airtight container for future use. Brewed green tea will be green to yellow in color and mildly astringent.

Here is what a handful of rolled tea leaves looks like.

BLACK TEA

Black tea is made from oxidized leaves of the *Camellia sinensis* var. *assamica* plant. During oxidation, oxygen causes the tea leaves to turn dark brown to black, giving black tea its signature bold, rich flavor. To make black tea, pick the leaf bud and top two leaves on the plant and follow these steps.

Wither: Place the fresh leaves on a screen (to allow airflow) and leave them out for at least twenty-four hours.

Roll: Roll the leaves between your palms to shape them. Working the leaves into tight balls or tubes releases the moisture, turning the leaves brown.

Oxidize: Spread the leaves out on a baking dish in a single layer. Leave them out to be exposed to oxygen. Room temperature, around 70°F (21°C), is ideal. Leave them out for two or more hours until the leaves turn brown.

Dry: Place the oxidized leaves in an oven preheated to 245°F (118°C) for fifteen to twenty minutes. The leaves should become brittle.

Sip: Add 1 teaspoon (5ml) of buds to a cup of boiling water and let steep for three to five minutes. DIY black tea is much weaker than commercial brews, so you might need a longer steep time than you're used to. Strain the buds before sipping.

OOLONG TEA

Oolong tea falls between black tea and green tea. How close it is to either depends on the tea master; some are more or less oxidized than others before the leaves are rolled. The steps to make oolong tea are similar to the steps used to make green and black tea. Pick the leaf bud and top two leaves on the plant and follow these steps.

Wither: Place fresh leaves on a screen and leave them out until the leaves start to turn brown.

Roll: Roll the leaves between your palms to shape them. Working the leaves into tight balls or tubes releases the moisture, turning the leaves brown.

Oxidize: Spread the leaves out on a baking dish in a single layer. Leave them out to be exposed to oxygen. Room temperature, around 70°F (21°C), is ideal. For tea with a lighter flavor that is closer to green tea, let them oxidize for up to ten hours; for a bolder flavor that is closer to black tea, let the leaves wither for twenty-four hours.

Dry: Place the oxidized leaves in an oven preheated to 245°F (118°C) for fifteen to twenty minutes. The leaves should become brittle.

Sip: Add 1 teaspoon (5ml) of leaves to a cup of boiling water and let steep for one to three minutes. Strain the leaves before sipping.

THYME
(*Thymus vulgaris*)
■ ZONES: 5 TO 9

Thyme is a small plant with mighty flavor. The small, oval, blue-green leaves have a flavor that has been described as a cross between mint, citrus, and pine; thyme has a strong mint fragrance. For the best flavor, harvest the aromatic leaves right before the plants flower.

This annual ground cover, known as garden thyme or common thyme, pairs well with other types of thyme, including lemon thyme (*Thymus × citriodorus*) and other mint species.

Native to Europe and parts of Asia and Africa, thyme grows up to 15 inches (38cm) tall and remains evergreen in warmer climates. Bees and butterflies love the pale purple flowers that bloom from May to July.

Thyme is considered a low-maintenance annual that tolerates drought and nutrient-poor soils; if the soil gets too wet, the herb could get root rot. Plant thyme in full sun and trim the stems as needed to prevent them from getting too woody.

Both fresh and dried thyme are associated with health benefits such as relieving menstrual cramps, easing indigestion,

aiding sleep, and preventing infections. Thymol, the active ingredient, is an antioxidant. Ingesting too much thyme can cause vomiting and nausea, and thyme isn't recommended for pregnant women because of the risk of miscarriage.

In Your Glass:

Make "country thyme" lemonade with fresh thyme, lemon juice, and sugar, or use it as the featured ingredient in cocktails. Pair with lemon, lime, or mint to enhance the flavor. You can also add thyme to the garden whiskey sour (see the recipe on page 129).

WITCH HAZEL
(*Hamamelis virginiana*)

■ **ZONES:** 3 TO 8

Witch hazel is both ornamental and medicinal. The shrub is a showstopper during the fall, when the leaves turn brilliant shades of gold and flowers with petals that look like thin yellow ribbons emerge. The fragrant flowers bloom between October and December, often clinging to the branches long after the leaves drop. Seeds appear after the flowers die and provide an important food source for wildlife.

The low-maintenance deciduous shrub grows up to 20 feet (6.1m) tall. Witch hazel will grow in partial shade, but the blooms are better if it's planted in full sun and moist, acidic soil. *H. virginiana* is the only witch hazel that blooms in the fall; vernal species (such as *H. vernalis*) bloom in the spring.

Both the leaves and bark are used in topical treatments to soothe sensitive skin.

As a medicinal herb, witch hazel treats inflammation, sore throats, colds, and the flu.

 *In Your Glass:*

The leaves and bark can be used to make tea. Use a sharp knife to strip small patches of bark from the tree before the leaves emerge in the spring. Cut the bark into small pieces and add 1 cup (240ml) of fresh bark or ½ cup (120ml) of dried bark to 2 cups (480ml) of boiling water and let steep for forty-five minutes. To make tea from witch hazel leaves, add 1 tablespoon (15ml) of fresh leaves or ½ tablespoon (7.5ml) of dried leaves to 1 cup (240ml) of boiling water and let it steep for twenty minutes. Strain the bark or leaves before sipping.

YAUPON

(*Ilex vomitoria*)

■ **ZONES:** 7 TO 9

Yaupon is a broadleaf evergreen that is believed to be the only plant native to North America that contains caffeine. Research shows that the 'Nana' cultivar has as much caffeine as green tea; adding nitrogen fertilizer can increase caffeine content up to 265 percent. Yaupon is a member of the

holly family, and some kinds of holly are poisonous, so be sure to only make tea from *Ilex vomitoria*.

Native Americans drank yaupon tea as a ceremonial drink. While yaupon fell out of favor as both a tea and a medicinal plant, Native Americans continued to grow the shrub as an ornamental. It grows up to 20 feet (6.1m) tall and 12 feet (3.7m) wide and has glossy green leaves that provide color year-round. Grow yaupon in full sun to part shade and moist soil. Both a male and female plant are required to bear small red berries that ripen in late fall. Birds love the berries, but the fruit isn't required to make tea.

Yaupon has about the same levels of antioxidants as blueberries. The tea is used to control blood pressure, aid digestion, ease constipation, reduce inflammation, and boost the immune system. It's not recommended for those with heart issues or women who are pregnant.

In Your Glass:

Yaupon tea is more complicated to brew than herbal infusions because the leaves need to be roasted first. Place a thin layer of freshly harvested yaupon leaves on a baking sheet and heat them in the oven preheated to 350°F (175°C) until the leaves start to turn brown (about fifteen minutes). Once the leaves cool, use a mortar and pestle to grind them into a fine texture. Add 1 tablespoon (15ml) of dried leaves to 1 cup (240ml) of water. Bring water to a boil and let simmer for at least five minutes. The longer it steeps, the stronger the flavor. Strain the leaves before drinking. Excess tea can be stored in a sealed jar. Yaupon tea has a slight bitterness and is similar in flavor to green tea.

Flowers

CALENDULA
(*Calendula officinalis*)
■ **ZONES:** 2 TO 11

The brightly colored flowers and long bloom times make calendula popular garden annuals. Different types of calendula, also known as pot marigold, produce single and double daisy-like flowers in a range of hues from light yellow to deep orange. The color—and the plant's popularity as a dye—earned calendula the nickname "poor man's saffron."

Calendula blooms from May through August; removing dead flowers can encourage subsequent blooms. The annual, which can survive as a perennial in zones 8

and higher, prefers cooler climates. Grow in full sun—part shade in warmer climates—and well-drained soil. Calendula can grow 1 foot (30cm) tall and 2 feet (60cm) wide. Cutting back the plants will encourage bushier growth.

Cultivated around the world for medicinal use, calendula is both anti-inflammatory and antimicrobial. It's used to calm upset stomachs, alleviate heartburn and acid reflux, ease sore throats, and combat respiratory infections. Calendula can stimulate menstruation, so pregnant women shouldn't consume it.

Add color to dishes like soups and salads with fresh flower petals. The edible flowers have flavors ranging from bitter to peppery. Calendula pairs well with rose hips (*Rosa rugosa*), safflower (*Carthamus tinctorius*), and all kinds of mint. Though you can dry calendula petals, the flavor is best in fresh flowers.

 *In Your Glass:*

Calendula tea is popular, but it is also a great addition to cocktails—there is even a cultivar called 'Citrus Cocktail.' Use it to make brightly colored simple syrup that can be used in a variety of cocktails, including margaritas (follow the recipe for mint simple syrup on page 125, substituting the mint with these colorful flowers).

CHAMOMILE
(*Matricaria recutita*)

■ **ZONES: 2 to 8**

Chamomile might be the most popular herbal tea. It's made from the daisy-like flowers of the German chamomile plant. The flowers, with yellow centers and white petals, bloom from June through August. Dried flower heads are used to make chamomile tea. (The stems smell great but are too bitter to use in tea.)

The word *chamomile* is of Greek origin and means "apple on the ground." The herb was named for its apple-like aroma and flavor. With mild sedative properties that aid in relaxation, the soothing herbal tea is often recommended as a sleep aid. Chamomile tea also helps with colds and flu, headaches, and stomach upset. Citrus-flavored herbs such as lemon balm and lemon verbena are great complements to chamomile.

German chamomile, also known as sweet false chamomile, is as ornamental as it is flavorful. Native to Western Europe, the plants grow up to 2 feet (60cm) tall. For optimal growth, do not

overwater. Chamomile will tolerate poor soils. Although it's considered an annual, chamomile might self-seed and return to the garden for subsequent seasons. Plants are easy to grow from seed.

Roman chamomile (*Chamaemelum nobile*) is a more petite species of chamomile. Although it's slightly more bitter and less sweet than German chamomile, it still makes flavorful herbal tea.

In Your Glass:

Chamomile is best known as an ingredient in herbal tea. To make chamomile tea, add 1 tablespoon (15ml) of dried chamomile flowers to 1 cup (240ml) of boiling water. Steep for at least five minutes; strain the flowers before sipping.

DANDELION

(*Taraxacum officinale*)

■ **ZONES:** 2 TO 10

Dandelions are among the first signs of spring, their bright yellow flower heads popping up among blades of grass, between cracks in the sidewalk, and along roadsides. These "weeds" are a staple of Chinese medicine, and tinctures made from the roots, leaves, and flowers are used to make restorative tonics. Dandelions contain vitamin C, fiber, potassium, beta-carotene, and protein. They are used to help with digestion and liver function and to fight off colds and the flu. All parts of the plant are also used in salads, wine, and tea.

Dandelions aren't typically cultivated in the garden so much as killed for having the nerve to push through the soil. Rather than purchasing the perennial herb at garden centers or ordering seeds through seed catalogs or online, dandelions are best harvested in the wild. Look for places off the beaten path that likely have not been sprayed with chemical weed killers. Eating dandelion greens has become so mainstream that some upscale supermarkets, including Whole Foods, stock them in the produce department.

Unlike the leaves, which have a bitter flavor, the flowers are sweet. Younger leaves are less bitter than more established leaves.

You can use all parts of the dandelion, fresh or dried. Since the flowers and leaves have different tastes, use them as separate herbs rather than adding both to a single brew. Consider adding sweeter herbs, like mint or lemon balm, to dandelion tea to offset the bitterness in the leaves. Serve dandelion tea hot or iced.

 *In Your Glass:*

Dandelion roots, once dried and roasted, can be used to make a coffee-like drink. To roast the roots, harvest and wash them well, cut them into pieces, place them on parchment paper, and put them in the oven at 200°F (93°C). Roast until the roots snap easily; this might take several hours. Cool and store in a sealed jar. To use, grind the roots and add them to coffee grounds at a 1:1 ratio. The common weed can also be used to make hot or iced tea. Separate the dandelion petals from the base of the flower. Pour boiling water over ½ cup (120ml) of dandelion petals and let steep for twenty minutes. (The flowers have a delicate flavor that requires a longer steep time to appreciate.) For dandelion leaf tea, add 4 tablespoons (60ml) of dandelion leaves to 1 cup (240ml) of boiling water and let steep for five minutes; add sweetener to taste. Consider adding sweeter herbs like mint or lemon balm to dandelion tea to offset the bitterness in the leaves. Dandelion tea can be served hot or iced.

ECHINACEA
(*Echinacea purpurea*)

■ **ZONES:** 3 TO 9

A staple in herbal medicine, echinacea is revered for its ability to fight infections, including colds and the flu. This perennial contains vitamins A, B, and E as well as minerals, including calcium and iron. All parts of the plant—leaves, flowers, and roots—are used in both herbal medicine and tea.

Echinacea is actually a genus, but it is used as a common noun to refer to several different species, which are also referred to as coneflowers. *E. purpurea*, native to the eastern United States, is called purple coneflower. Yellow coneflower (*E. paradoxa*) is native to Arkansas, Missouri, Oklahoma, and Texas and produces yellow flowers. Tennessee coneflower (*E. tennesseensis*) is, as

its name suggests, native to Tennessee, and it also produces purple blooms.

Coneflowers are as pretty as they are practical. *E. purpurea* is a perennial that produces flowers with daisy-like purple petals radiating from prominent conical orange centers that bloom from June to August. If you don't remove the flowers, the

seed heads will blacken and attract birds in search of a nutritious meal; the nectar-rich flowers are favorites of bees and butterflies. Japanese beetles also love echinacea and make fast work of defoliating the plants. Leaving seed heads intact allows for vigorous self-seeding.

Grow echinacea in full sun to part shade and well-drained soil. This heat- and drought-tolerant herb grows well in poor soil. Echinacea will grow up to 5 feet (1.5m) tall. The colorful blooms make excellent cut flowers.

In Your Glass:

Although echinacea is best known as a popular herb for tea, the flowers can also be used in juice. Add mint or citrus-flavored herbs, such as lemon verbena, to help minimize the astringent taste. To make the tea, add 2 teaspoons (10ml) of fresh flowers or 1 teaspoon (5ml) of dried flowers to 2 cups (480ml) of boiling water and steep for five minutes.

HIBISCUS
(*Hibiscus rosa-sinensis*)

■ **ZONES:** 9 TO 11

The bright blooms on these tropical beauties command attention. Chinese hibiscus is one of a number of hibiscus varieties grown for their evergreen leaves and saucer-sized flowers. The single or double blossoms can reach up to 8 inches (20cm) in diameter and come in shades ranging from white, light pink, and apricot to red and orange. Hibiscus flowers often last just one day, so pluck them immediately to use in tea.

Chinese hibiscus, also called China rose, rose mallow, and Hawaiian hibiscus, grows up to 10 feet (3.1m) tall. Below zone 10, hibiscus needs to be overwintered indoors. Other species, such as *H. lasiocarpos*, will survive the winters in colder climates.

Plant in full sun to part shade and in a location protected from strong winds; keep soil moist. Chinese hibiscus is sensitive to changes in its environment. Shifts in temperature, humidity, light, and soil moisture can cause leaves to yellow or drop.

Tea brewed with the antioxidant-rich flowers and leaves has been shown to lower blood pressure, increase HDL (aka "good") cholesterol, and fight infections, such as bronchitis. Some studies have also found that drinking hibiscus tea aids weight loss.

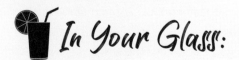 *In Your Glass:*

These flowers turn the water a lovely pink hue, making hibiscus tea feel like a festive brew. Hibiscus tea has a tart flavor, so cut it with lemon or lime juice; adding honey also adds sweetness. Prepare hibiscus tea hot or iced. Hibiscus can also be used to make a simple syrup (see the recipe on page 125); add it to sangria or cocktails made with champagne.

JASMINE
(*Jasminum officinale*)
■ **ZONES:** 7 TO 10

Jasmine tea has been around since 1300 AD. The fragrant and flavorful tea is so time consuming to prepare that it was once reserved for royalty. Tea leaves and jasmine flowers are harvested at different times, so, in traditional preparation, tea leaves were harvested and stored until the jasmine flowers bloomed, and then the fresh flowers were layered with green tea until the leaves absorbed the perfume from the flowers. Some of the most prized varieties of jasmine tea repeat the process multiple times for a tea that has a floral flavor and heady scent.

 **In Your Glass:**

Use the fragrant flowers to make tea. In a glass jar, add ½ cup (120ml) of fresh jasmine flowers to 1 cup (240ml) of dried loose-leaf green tea, sandwiching the green tea between layers of flowers. Seal the jar and let it sit for at least twenty-four hours. Shake the jar to mix the flowers and tea leaves. To brew, add 1 teaspoon (5ml) of jasmine tea to 1 cup (240ml) of boiling water and let it steep for at least five minutes. Strain the tea before serving.

Growing the vine is much easier than making traditional jasmine tea. Jasmine prefers full sun to part shade and can grow up to 15 feet (4.6m) wide and twice as tall. The fast-growing vine needs a trellis or other support. A profusion of fragrant blooms appears from April to September. Jasmine should be pruned after flowering to control its rapid growth. Pollinators love the nectar-rich, tubular flowers that are white to pale pink.

The deciduous vine has been associated with health benefits, such as lowering cholesterol, reducing the risk of heart attack, improving the immune system, easing inflammation, and preventing diabetes. Because jasmine is acidic, drinking too much jasmine tea may cause stomach upset.

LAVENDER
(*Lavandula angustifolia*)
■ **ZONES:** 5 TO 8

Although Provence is famous for its colorful fields of lavender, the fragrant perennial is not native to France. Despite it being commonly called English lavender, it's not native to England, either. Lavender hails from the Mediterranean. (French lavender, *Lavandula dentata*, is also from the Mediterranean.)

Lavender is an herbaceous perennial that grows in upright clumps. Long shoots of purple flowers bloom atop narrow gray-green leaves. It's best suited to full sun and well-drained soil, but it will tolerate poor soil and drought. Keep stems from turning woody by aggressively pruning plants after bloom; thin annually.

There are several different cultivars of English lavender. 'Hidcote' is known for its dark purple flower spikes; it has a fruitier flavor than other kinds of lavender. 'Lavenite Petite' hails from New Zealand and produces pom-pom-like flower spikes. 'Miss Katherine' is one of a few pink types of lavender and has elegant sprays of deep pink blooms. All lavender species can be used in tea.

Lavender is prized for its fragrance, making it a popular ingredient in soaps, bath oils, and perfumes. Thanks to the healing effects of its essential oils, the plant has a long history of use in folk medicine for a range of ailments, including insomnia, depression, chronic pain, muscle spasms, digestion, inflammation, and stress. Too much lavender can trigger side effects like nausea and vomiting.

Lavender is related to both mint and rosemary; the taste is often described as a marriage of those flavors. While the flavor is pleasing to most, some perceive the taste as soapy. With its spicy floral flavor—with hints of mint and lemon—lavender is excellent when paired with chamomile, lemon-flavored herbs, or bergamot, the orange-flavored herb that gives Earl Grey its distinctive flavor.

 *In Your Glass:*

The color and flavor of lavender make it a go-to ingredient in a broad range of drinks, from tea and lemonade to martinis. It also makes an excellent simple syrup. Try the recipe for lavender simple syrup on page 125 or the lavender lemonade recipe on page 140 to see how this beautiful, fragrant perennial transforms your favorite drinks.

PURPLE PASSIONFLOWER

(Passiflora incarnata)

■ ZONES: 5 TO 9

Spanish conquistadors believed that the unusual-looking passionflower signified the Passion of Christ, the center of the flower being suggestive of the crown of thorns that Jesus wore during the crucifixion. Lore aside, passionflower is regarded as a powerful sedative, effective for treating insomnia, anxiety, attention deficit/hyperactivity disorder, and chronic pain. Those on antidepressants or antianxiety medications should not ingest passionflower.

There are more than 400 species in the genus *Passiflora*. *P. incarnata*, which is native to the eastern United States, is the hardiest of all passionflowers; other species, such as red passionflower (*P. coccinea*) and blue passionflower (*P. caerulea*), both native to Central and South America, require more tropical conditions to thrive and will do best in zones 9 and higher. The flowers, leaves, and stems of all species of passionflower can be used in teas.

Passionflower grows up to 8 feet (2.4m) tall and 6 feet (1.8m) wide; the vine will climb a support, like a trellis, if provided. Choose a location in full sun to part shade. The flowers have long, narrow, white petals with tricolored filaments in dark purple, lavender, and white; the centers have chartreuse stamens and purple stigmas. Passionflower blooms from July to September. The flowers have a mild, earthy flavor. Edible fruits, known as maypops for the popping sound they make when stepped on, appear in July; maypops can be eaten fresh from the vine or made into preserves.

The fast-growing vine spreads via root suckers and can take over a garden. Prune at the beginning of spring, cutting back stems to their base. Passionflower might not survive the winter in cold climates.

In Your Glass:

To make tea from purple passionflower, mix 1 tablespoon (15ml) of fresh leaves and flowers or 1 teaspoon (5ml) of dried leaves and flowers with 1 cup (240ml) of boiling water and let steep for at least five minutes. The longer the tea steeps, the more complex the flavor becomes; it takes on a richer, almost toasted, flavor with a hint of bitterness. The beautiful flowers can also be used as a garnish.

RED CLOVER

(*Trifolium pratense*)

■ **ZONES:** 3 TO 10

Bees love these sweet perennial weeds that pop up in lawns in the spring. Red clover is a fast-growing ground cover with bright pink flowers that appear like globes in the grass. Rather than breaking out the herbicides at the first sign of red clover, take a cue from the bees, who enjoy the flowers' sweet flavor.

Red clover also has myriad medicinal benefits. It is used to treat high cholesterol, respiratory infections, asthma, and indigestion, and to help prevent cancer. The flowers contain isoflavones that the body converts to phytoestrogens similar to estrogen, making red clover a popular herb to alleviate the symptoms of premenstrual syndrome and menopause, including hot flashes. Because red clover acts like estrogen, it should be avoided during pregnancy and breastfeeding.

The herbaceous perennials are ubiquitous in lawns, along roadsides,

and in fields. They are widely considered weeds, so most garden centers don't sell red clover, but seeds are available. Beware that red clover can be aggressive; the stems send out nodules that creep through the grass, and a single plant can spread up to 12 inches (30cm). Planting it in containers and pruning it after it blooms will help control its spread. Plant in full sun to part shade; red clover blooms in May and June.

Farmers often use red clover and white clover (*T. repens*) for crop rotation because both are nitrogen fixers that add nitrogen back to the soil. When foraging for red clover, choose sites that haven't been sprayed with herbicides or pesticides.

 *In Your Glass:*

There is a cocktail called red clover, but it's made with vodka, lemon juice, simple syrup, raspberries, and egg whites, and not a trace of the perennial weed. Instead, use red clover to make tea. Add 2 tablespoons (30ml) of fresh flowers or 1 tablespoon (15ml) of dried flowers to 1 cup (240ml) of boiling water and let steep for ten minutes. Strain the flowers before drinking.

TRUMPET HONEYSUCKLE
(*Lonicera sempervirens*)

■ **ZONES: 4 to 9**

Most of the 180 species of honeysuckle originated in Asia, but trumpet honeysuckle, not to be confused with trumpet vine, is native to the southeastern United States. The vines are vigorous growers, reaching 15 feet (4.6m) tall and 6 feet (1.8m) wide. If not supported by a trellis, the vines become dense ground cover.

Trumpet honeysuckle produces tubular scarlet flowers with orange and yellow insides in May and June. Nectar-seeking critters like birds, hummingbirds, and butterflies love the tubular flowers. While some honeysuckle has a heady scent, trumpet honeysuckle produces no discernible fragrance. The flowers have a delicate flavor. Pluck them after bloom for tea. The mild flavor almost disappears when the flowers are dried; use fresh flowers instead. Do not consume the red berries that appear in late summer and early fall.

The perennial vine, which is semi-deciduous in zones 8 and higher, should be pruned after bloom. Aggressive pruning can keep growth in check. Grow trumpet honeysuckle in full sun and moist, well-drained soil.

If you venture away from *Lonicera sempervirens*, be careful to choose the right species of honeysuckle for the garden. Both bush honeysuckle (*L. maackii*) and Japanese honeysuckle (*L. japonica*) are destructive invasive species that take over landscapes and choke out other plants.

All kinds of honeysuckle are known for their ability to reduce inflammation, ease upper respiratory infections such as colds and the flu, treat urinary tract infections, alleviate headaches, and help with digestive disorders. The pretty vine can also slow blood clotting and should be avoided before and after surgeries.

In Your Glass:

The sweet taste is popular in iced tea and lemonade. (Avoid using honeysuckle in hot tea, as boiling water can cause the flowers to taste bitter.) Gently crush fresh honeysuckle flowers to release their flavor. Mix 1 cup (240ml) of dried flowers with 2 cups (480ml) of cold water. Stir and cover. Leave the mixture in the refrigerator overnight; strain the flowers and pour over ice to serve.

TUFTED VIOLET

(*Viola cornuta*)

■ **ZONES:** 6 TO 11

The bloom of these petite flowers signals the arrival of spring. These tender perennials appear as early as March and remain in bloom throughout the summer, often flowering a second time in the fall. In hot climates, flowers might fade, but they can make a comeback in the fall. Plant in full sun or part shade.

Tufted violets are among 550 species in the *Viola* genus. Also known as pansies or Johnny jump-ups, violets are the state flowers for four US states: Illinois, New Jersey, Rhode Island, and Wisconsin.

The tufted violet, also known as the horned violet, is a perennial that grows up to 8 inches (20cm) tall. Different varieties produce different-colored flowers; most are two-toned in shades of blue, violet, lavender, yellow, orange, peach, and white (similar to pansies). The sweet violet (*Viola odorata*) is one of few tufted violets planted for its fragrance.

Research shows that violet leaves are chock full of vitamins. In fact, the leaves have as much vitamin C as an orange and similar vitamin A content to spinach. Harvest flowers and leaves throughout the season, but do not eat the roots; they can cause diarrhea. Use both fresh and dried leaves to make tea. Violets are used to treat a range of ailments, from headaches and congestion to sore throats and fevers.

 *In Your Glass:*

Violet simple syrup adds a sweet flavor and lovely purple color to cocktails. You can also use the flowers to make tea by adding 2 tablespoons (30ml) of fresh or dried (chopped) flowers to 1 cup (240ml) of boiling water. Let the tea steep for ten minutes and strain before drinking.

Fruits and Vegetables

BEET
(*Beta vulgaris*)
■ **ZONES:** 2 TO 11

This cool-weather vegetable falls into four different groups of cultivars. The most common, garden beets, are the familiar root vegetables grown in the garden and sold in the supermarket produce section. Lesser-known groups include the sugar beet group, containing cultivars that are grown for sugar; the fodder beet group, with tubers harvested for livestock fodder; and the leaf beet group, which includes chard and spinach beets that are grown for their edible leaves.

Beets are believed to have evolved from a North African root vegetable. The first recorded cultivation of garden beets for their roots dates back to 1542, but their leaves were eaten long before the bulbous roots became popular.

 **In Your Glass:**

Beets are an excellent base for juice. Raw beets are bitter. Mix with sweet ingredients like lemon, apple, and pineapple to improve the flavor; ginger and carrots also pair well with beets. Try the recipe for veggie juice on page 141.

The annual vegetable grows best in moist, fertile soil and full sun, but beets will also tolerate light shade. In zones 3 to 7, sow seeds before the last spring frost and harvest

the deep purple root vegetables in summer and fall. Seeds can be sown in summer in zones 8 to 10 and harvested over the winter.

Beets do more than just add flavor and color to drinks like juices, shrubs, and martinis. The root vegetables are a good source of potassium, fiber, folate, and vitamin C; beets also contain nitrates, compounds that have been associated with lower blood pressure and increased stamina.

BLACKBERRY
(*Rubus* sp.)

■ **ZONES:** 6 TO 8

Blackberries, plucked straight from the vine, are one of the highlights of summer. You can use fresh or frozen fruit in cocktails, lemonade, and infused waters; to make great tea, though, look to the leaves. Although the flavor of blackberry leaves is mild (and a little sweet), the leaves contain antioxidants, vitamin C, and tannins.

The bushes, available in erect or trailing and thorny or thornless varieties, are great fruit-bearing plants for beginning gardeners. The easy-to-grow plants grow best in full sun and acidic, moist—but not wet—soil. Trailing blackberries, such as 'Olallie,' need a trellis for support. Blackberries self-pollinate, which means that you don't need multiple bushes for fruit production.

The erect, thornless cultivar 'Navaho' produces an abundance of mature fruit in July. 'Illini Hardy' also produces fruit in July; the erect and thorny cultivar is winter hardy and thrives in colder climates.

Mature blackberries are firm and black in color. Harvest them in the morning or evening, when temperatures are cooler, and refrigerate your take after picking. You can use both fresh and dried leaves in tea. Fermenting the leaves brings out their flavor. To ferment, crush wilted leaves, wrap them in a damp cloth, and store them in a warm, dark area for seventy-two hours. Remove the leaves from the cloth and dry them before brewing.

Thanks to their high antioxidant content, blackberries are known for lowering cholesterol and reducing the risk of cardiovascular disease; the berries are also high in vitamin C, calcium, potassium, and magnesium.

In Your Glass:

Add blackberries to lemonade or use the fruits to add sweetness to cocktails and mocktails like mojitos, margaritas, and whiskey sours. The fruit pairs well with lime, basil, clove, vanilla, and other berries and citrus flavors. For tea, add 1 teaspoon (5ml) of fermented blackberry leaves (see instructions above) to 2 cups (480ml) of boiling water and steep for three to five minutes. Strain the leaves before sipping.

BLACK CURRANT

(Ribes nigrum)

■ **ZONES:** 3 to 7

Black currant is an underappreciated fruit. In spring, after the chartreuse flowers are spent, fruits appear. The bunches of green berries ripen to glossy black fruits starting in June. The flavor of black currants has been described as fresh and floral with notes of raspberries; the fruit is tart.

The berries are high in antioxidants, polyphenols, and gamma-linolenic acid, an omega-6 fatty acid that reduces inflammation. Black currants have four times more vitamin C than oranges and twice the antioxidants of blueberries. As a medicinal plant, black currant is used to boost the immune system, ease flu symptoms, and reduce joint and muscle pain and stiffness. Both fresh and dried berries and leaves can be used in your favorite drinks.

The compact bushes grow up to 4 feet (1.2m) tall and wide. It can take up to five years before the plants produce fruit. Black currant grows best in sun to part shade and moist, fertile soil. The self-fertile plants require regular pruning during the dormant season. Diseases and pests are an issue with black currant; plants are prone to gall mites, powdery mildew, and black currant leaf midge, which can affect growth and fruit production.

 *In Your Glass:*

To make black currant tea, add 2 teaspoons (10ml) of dried berries to 2 cups (480ml) of boiling water and steep for thirty minutes. The berries are safe to eat and can remain in the tea, or you can strain and set them aside.

BLOOD ORANGE

(*Citrus × sinensis*)

■ **ZONES:** 9 TO 11

Blood oranges, named for the color of their flesh, are citrus fruits, but they have a sweet flavor similar to fresh berries. The hybrid, which is believed to be a deliberate cross between a hybrid mandarin orange (*Citrus reticulata*) and a hybrid pomelo (*Citrus maxima*), originated in Asia.

Although the tropical fruit trees grow best in traditional citrus-growing regions like California, Texas, and Florida, blood oranges are cold (but not frost) tolerant and can survive outdoors in cooler climates. The broadleaf evergreen trees can be overwintered indoors in a south-facing window. Mature trees can reach heights of up to 20 feet (6m).

Blood orange trees produce medium-sized, easy-to-peel fruits; the color of their sweet flesh ranges from yellow and orange to deep red and dark purple. Fruits mature between December and February; the tree often bears fruit in alternating years. The sweet fruits are the main attraction, but blood orange trees also produce fragrant white flowers in the spring.

For easier overwintering, plant blood orange trees in pots with slightly acidic, sandy soil. Do not overwater; too much moisture can make the trees more susceptible to diseases such as stem-end rot.

 *In Your Glass:*

Blood oranges add both color and flavor to drinks such as margaritas, martinis, cosmopolitans, fruit punches, and juice. Balance the sweet, slightly tart flavor with apricot, ginger, clove, or honey. To make a fizzy, fruity brunch cocktail, mix ½ cup (120ml) of juice from blood oranges with 1 bottle (750ml) of prosecco and ¼ cup (60ml) of simple syrup.

CARROT

(*Daucus carota* var. *sativus*)

■ **ZONES:** 2 TO 11

This popular vegetable is not just for salads. Carrots are edible taproots that were believed to grow wild in Afghanistan before being introduced as cultivated vegetables in North America.

Different subtypes of carrots produce vegetables in different sizes and shapes. For long, slender carrots, grow Nantes and Imperator carrots; the Chantenay and Danvers subtypes produce squat, rounded carrots. The 'Gold Pak' carrot produces a taproot that can reach up to 10 inches (25cm) long and has a slightly sweet flavor, while small, round 'Atlas' carrots produce rounded taproots up to 2 inches (5cm) in diameter. In addition to conventional orange carrots, consider "rainbow" carrots that come in colors like dark purple, red, yellow, and even white.

Grow carrots in full sun and loose, fertile soil. Seeds can be sown in spring and fall. It can take up to four months for carrots to mature. Carrots are biennial; leave them in the soil and the plants will flower and produce seeds next season. The cool-weather crop can succumb to bacterial diseases like vegetable soft rot in hot, humid weather.

For the best flavor, eat (and drink) carrots right after harvesting. The nutrient-dense vegetable is high in fiber, potassium, and vitamins C and K.

 *In Your Glass:*

Add carrots to the blender for a healthy juice (see the recipe on page 141). The savory flavor pairs well with ingredients like citrus, honey, and ginger. Carrots are also a creative cocktail ingredient that can be mixed with a splash of whiskey or vodka.

CELERY

(*Apium graveolens*)

■ **ZONES:** 3 TO 6

Celery is often relegated to garnish status, but the crunchy vegetable has potential beyond the Bloody Mary.

There are three types of celery, and each is grown for a different purpose. Stalk celery (*Apium graveolens* var. *dulce*) is, as its name suggests, grown for its crunchy stalks. It is the most common type of celery grown in US gardens. Celeraic or root celery (*Apium graveolens* var. *rapaceum*) is a root vegetable similar to a turnip. Finally, leaf celery (*Apium graveolens* var. *secalinum*) is a leafier version of stalk celery cultivated for its seeds, which are used as spices in parts of Asia.

Long before the vegetable was cultivated for food, wild celery was used for medicinal purposes ranging from improved digestion and reduced blood pressure to lowered inflammation. In the 1600s, the French began growing celery for food, and it became prized for its sweet stalks.

The cool-weather vegetable is native to Mediterranean climates in Europe, Asia, and Africa and often struggles in hot, humid locations. Even in the best conditions, celery can be difficult to grow. Choose a sunny location with well-drained soil and keep the crop well watered (but not too wet; too much moisture can lead to root rot). Watch for pests like aphids, earwigs, slugs, and celery worms. It takes up to four months before the stalks are mature enough to harvest.

In Your Glass:

Celery juice is popular as a low-calorie health drink, but juice made solely from the stalks can be hard to swallow. Add apple, ginger, and lemon juice to improve the flavor. To make a healthy, sweet juice, mix 2 celery stalks, chopped, to 1 tart apple (like Granny Smith or Honeycrisp), cut into chunks, and 2 teaspoons (10ml) of fresh ginger, chopped. Put all of this into a juicer and add 2 tablespoons (30ml) of lemon juice.

CUCUMBER
(*Cucumis sativus*)

■ **ZONES:** 2 TO 11

Cucumbers are members of the gourd family, Cucurbitaceae, which includes watermelon, squash, pumpkin, and muskmelon. Although there are more than 100 different cucumber cultivars, pickling, slicing, and seedless are the most common in American gardens.

Slicing and pickling cucumbers contain seeds; stick with seedless cultivars for beverages. English cucumbers—the long, thin vegetables sold in supermarkets wrapped in plastic—are the most popular seedless cucumber. 'Unistar' and 'Iznik' are also easy-to-grow, tasty options for the garden.

Cucumbers are native to Asia and grow best in hot climates. Wait until temperatures reach 70°F (21°C) before planting the frost-tender seedlings in the garden. Choose a location with full sun and fertile soil. Bush cucumbers are more compact plants, but vining cucumbers, which can reach up to

8 feet (2.4m) in length, need lots of space to grow. In a small garden, train the vines to grow up a trellis or cage to save space. Avoid waiting too long to harvest: older cucumbers can be bitter, whereas younger fruits are tender and have better flavor.

 *In Your Glass:*

Add cucumbers to drinks made with basil, cilantro, mint, cantaloupe, and watermelon to bring out their flavor. Their mild, melon-like taste makes cucumbers ideal for infused water, *agua fresca*, margaritas, martinis, and even lemonade. Cucumbers can also be added to the special gin and tonic recipe on page 137.

KALE

(*Brassica oleracea*)

■ **ZONES:** 2 TO 11

In 2014, kale took the title of America's favorite leafy green. It showed up in everything from salads to pesto to tacos and, of course, kale chips, and earned "superfood" status because it's high in protein, fiber, and calcium and has tons of vitamins A, C, and K.

Like other vegetables in the *Brassica* genus, including kohlrabi, collard greens, and cauliflower, kale prefers cooler temperatures in spring and fall; the leaves start to wilt when temperatures rise above 80°F (26°C). Kale will tolerate cold temperatures, and the leaves often taste best after a light frost. In milder climates, kale will continue producing all winter.

Kale is a low-maintenance vegetable. Choose a sunny spot in the garden, watch for pests like cabbageworms and slugs, and watch it grow. The light green to blue-green leaves can grow up to 18 inches (45cm) tall. Be sure to plant edible types such as curly kale, Ripbor kale, and Lacinto kale, rather than ornamental kale, which is grown for foliage in a range of colors from purple to pink to white but is not meant to be eaten.

In Your Glass:

Unlike other leafy greens, which tend to have strong flavors, kale is mild and has a hint of pepper. Kale is a popular smoothie ingredient and pairs well with oranges and other citrus fruits, pineapples, bananas, and blueberries. Add 2 cups (480ml) of fresh kale, chopped, to the smoothie recipe on page 142 for a nutrient boost.

MEYER LEMON

(*Citrus* × *meyeri*)

■ **ZONES:** 9 TO 11

One bite of a Meyer lemon is all it takes to recognize that the hard-to-grow citrus plant is worth the effort.

Once grown as a decorative houseplant, the Meyer lemon has become popular for its aromatic fragrance and sweet flavor. The fruit, a cross between a lemon (*Citrus limon*) and a mandarin orange (*Citrus reticulata*), adds subtle sweetness to lemonade, marmalade, and lemon bars. Meyer lemons are native to China and can be cultivated in citrus-growing regions such as Florida and California where temperatures hover around 70°F (21°C). It goes dormant if temperatures dip below 55°F (13°C). In cooler climates, Meyer lemons can be grown indoors as a houseplant.

Meyer lemons are tropical plants that thrive in full sun and produce pretty white flowers all year long in a mild climate. Choose a location that provides protection from wind. The broadleaf evergreen can grow up to 10 feet (3m) tall. Soil should be well drained, not moist. Indoor plants will need to be hand-pollinated to set fruit. Regular misting in the winter is essential.

Commercial cultivation of Meyer lemons is limited. The fruit is thin-skinned, making it hard to ship. Your best bet to get the sweet, tangy flavor is to grow the hybrid citrus tree in your garden. Meyer lemons lack the acidity of regular lemons, making them more palatable to eat raw.

In Your Glass:

Meyer lemons add a tart punch to the lavender lemonade recipe on page 140. But also think beyond lemonade and add these fruits to martinis and margaritas. Grate the zest from a Meyer lemon into an ice cube tray and fill with juice; the cubes can be added to infused water for an extra punch of flavor.

PERSIMMON

(*Diospyros virginiana*)

■ **ZONES:** 4 TO 9

Though persimmons in the species *Diospyros kaki* are native to China, the fruits are also grown across the United States, including natively in the species *Diospyros virginiana*. In the spring, persimmon trees produce fragrant white to light green flowers; fruit appears in the fall. They're

astringent before they ripen, but when the small reddish-orange fruits are at their peak, they are sweet and have a pudding-like texture. (Ripe fruit is not too firm or too soft. Pressing the flesh should leave a light indentation.)

Persimmons have a flavor similar to apricots, but the fruit, which is less than 2 inches (5cm) in diameter, is not a stone fruit; persimmons are berries. Of the common cultivars, *Diospyros kaki* 'Hachiya' is more astringent and has a strong, tart flavor unless the fruit is ripe, while *D. kaki* 'Fuyu' produces a sweeter, tomato-shaped fruit.

Persimmons are not the best choice for a small garden. The trees grow up to 60 feet (18m) tall and need room to spread their branches. Most species are dioecious, which means that each tree is either male or female. Pollination—and fruit set—requires a male and female tree.

These colorful fruits contain vitamins A, C, and E; fiber; manganese; and copper. Persimmons also contain antioxidants that are beneficial for heart health and inflammation and might help lower LDL (aka "bad") cholesterol.

 In Your Glass:

The leaves and fruit (fresh or dried) can be used in tea, juice, smoothies, and cocktails. The fruit, with its sweet, honey-like flavor, can be used with cinnamon, clove, citrus, apple, and ginger. Chop 5 persimmons and add to 3 cups (720ml) of white vinegar and 2 cups (480ml) of sugar to make a fruit shrub that can be added to club soda or ginger ale to make a delicious mocktail. The leaves have a mild, bittersweet flavor. Traditional teas are often blended with cinnamon, ginger, and turmeric.

RASPBERRY

(*Rubus idaeus*)

■ **ZONES:** 5 TO 8

Raspberries are the perfect combination of sweet and tart. The delicate red fruits are part of a group of fruits called brambles that produce berries on canes. Most varieties produce white (and sometimes pink or light purple) flowers in April; berries ripen in the summer. It takes a full year before the plants produce fruit. Red raspberries are the most common, but other varieties produce fruits that are black, purple, and yellow.

Plant raspberries in full sun to part shade. The healthiest canes grow in well-drained, acidic soil. Wet soil can cause root rot. Raspberries are vigorous growers that reach 3 to 9 feet (90cm to 2.6m) tall and spread up to 3 feet (90cm) wide. Without pruning, raspberries can grow into impenetrable thickets. Canes that produce berries—called fruiting canes—need to be pruned to the ground after the fruit is harvested. In the spring, cut canes back again, removing about 25 percent of the canes. Watch for thorns.

Although raspberries are grown for their fruit, the bright green leaves are also used in tea. Young leaves are the most flavorful. Harvest leaves in the spring before the fruit appears. Raspberry leaves taste like mild black tea.

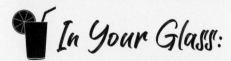 *In Your Glass:*

Raspberry lemonade is a summertime staple. Mix 1 cup (240ml) of fresh (pureed) raspberries, 2 cups (480ml) of lemon juice, 6 cups (1.4L) of water, and 1 cup (240ml) of sugar; strain the mixture through a sieve and serve over ice. You can add fresh raspberries to the glass for extra color and interest.

RHUBARB

(*Rheum rhabarbarum*)

■ **ZONES:** 3 TO 8

It might not be the most common vegetable, but this leafy green makes a great addition to a beverage garden. Rhubarb first appeared in American seed catalogs in 1829, but its cultivation dates back as far as the late 1200s, when it was grown in China for medicinal purposes. The root and rhizome are still used in Eastern medicine to alleviate digestive issues like heartburn and diarrhea.

The stalks, in colors such as green, pink, and deep red, are tart and acidic, making them an excellent addition to pies, jams, and sauces, as well as drinks such as lemonade and margaritas.

Rhubarb grows up to 3 feet (1m) tall and 4 feet (1.2m) wide. The leaf stalks are edible, with flavors ranging from tart to sweet, but the leaves contain oxalic acid, **which is toxi**c, so the leaves must be removed before eating.

The perennial plant thrives in cooler temperatures (and is grown as an annual in the southern United States). Grow rhubarb in full sun or part shade and slightly acidic soil. Wait until the second year to harvest the stalks and cut only those that are at least 12 inches (30cm) long. To ensure continued production, leave at least two stalks on each plant. Rhubarb can be split every three years.

 *In Your Glass:*

Rhubarb can be used in mojitos, simple syrup (see the recipe on page 125), lemonade, and soda. It pairs well with mint, strawberries, and ginger.

RUGOSA ROSE
(*Rosa rugosa*)

■ ZONES: 2 TO 7

More than 100 species of roses belong to the genus *Rosa*. Roses, often cultivated for their beautiful flowers, come in a range of colors and fragrances; some roses climb, others trail, and most have thorns on their stems. The deciduous shrubs grow best in full sun and moist, well-drained soil. Late-winter pruning helps promote vigorous growth.

The rugosa rose produces edible fruits known as rose hips. Rose hips sit just below the petals and contain the seeds for the rose plant. These small fruits form in late summer, after the roses have bloomed, and are an excellent source of vitamin C, making them popular for treating colds and flu. Rose hips are also used to treat inflammation, high blood pressure, high cholesterol, fever, and

digestive issues, including diarrhea and constipation. For health benefits, fresh rose hips are best because processing destroys the nutrients.

Rugosa rose is native to Asia. The deciduous shrub grows up to 6 feet (1.8m) tall and produces fragrant pink to white flowers; most have single petals, but some have semidouble or double petals. Without pruning, the rose throws out suckers and forms dense thickets. The stems are covered in sharp thorns. Like other species of rose, the rugosa rose is susceptible to several diseases, including black spot and powdery mildew, but is considered more disease resistant than most roses; disease resistance is improved when the roses are planted in full sun. Rugosa rose grows so well in coastal conditions, where it grows in sand dunes, that it has earned the nicknames "beach rose" and "salt spray rose."

In Your Glass:

You can make rose hip tea from both fresh and dried rose hips. It has a tart, fruity flavor. Rose hips are also popular in garden-to-glass cocktails. Make a simple syrup by boiling 4 cups (960ml) of rose hips with 2 cups (480ml) of water and 1 cup (240ml) of sugar. Or use the edible fruits to make cocktails, like a whiskey smash: add 1 ounce (30ml) of simple syrup to 2 ounces (60ml) of bourbon or whiskey and garnish with fresh mint. Rose hips have a sour taste; the rye whiskey in a whiskey smash will tone it down. Add sweeter herbs, like mint, when using rose hips in virgin drinks.

SPINACH

(Spinacia oleracea)

■ **ZONES:** 2 TO 11

Popeye isn't the only one who loved spinach; Europeans started growing the cool-weather vegetable in the 1400s. The leaves are chock-full of iron and vitamins A, B, and C, and, thanks to its "superfood" status, spinach is used in everything from salads and omelets to smoothies.

There are three different types of spinach: savoy, semi-savoy, and flat spinach (also called smooth leaf spinach). Savoy spinach has short, crinkled leaves; semi-savoy spinach leaves are taller and less crinkled; and smooth spinach, the most popular type of the leafy green, has flat leaves.

Spinach grows best in spring and fall. The leafy greens are cold hardy, and established plants will tolerate temperatures down to about 20 to 25°F (-7 to -4°C). In the heat of the summer, the plants will bolt (send up flower spikes and set seeds, halting leaf growth), leaving you without a crop. Some varieties do better in hot, humid temperatures than others. Malabar spinach (*Basella alba*) is native to tropical regions of Asia and thrives in the heat; it produces leaves with red stems that have a mild flavor similar to Swiss chard. Plant spinach in full sun to part shade and keep soil moist.

 *In Your Glass:*

Thanks to its nutrient content, spinach is popular in smoothies, but the strong flavor means you don't want to drink this leafy green solo. Add fruits like blueberries, strawberries, or bananas to add sweetness to a smoothie. Add 2 cups (480ml) of fresh spinach, chopped, to the smoothie recipe on page 142.

STAGHORN SUMAC

(*Rhus typhina*)

■ **ZONES:** 3 TO 8

Staghorn sumac, sometimes generally known as wild sumac, is best known for its bright red leaves and red berries that burst forth in the fall. The tree, which grows up to 25 feet (7.6m) tall, has rust-colored hairs covering its young branches, giving them a velvet-like texture. Leaves on the deciduous tree are bright green during spring and summer and transition to brilliant shades of red, orange, and yellow during the fall.

The berries on staghorn sumac, like the leaves, also have a fuzzy texture. The berries are juicy and have a tart citrus flavor, but, thanks to the texture, sumac berries are best spit out, not swallowed.

As its common name, wild sumac, suggests, staghorn sumac grows unbidden in woodlands and wetlands. It should not be confused with poison sumac (*Toxicodendron vernix*), a tree related to poison ivy and poison oak. Look at the

berries to distinguish staghorn sumac from its poisonous relative: staghorn sumac has deep red berries growing on upright stalks, whereas the berries on poison sumac are white and hang from the branches. If you are not sure which species the berries come from, do not eat them.

The plant is popular in Middle Eastern and Mediterranean cooking. Thanks to high levels of antioxidants and vitamin C, Native Americans used sumac berries to treat colds, the flu, and scurvy. Research has shown that sumac berries help reduce blood sugar in those with type 2 diabetes.

In Your Glass:

The berries can be used to make tea. Pick several clusters of berries and crush them to release the flavor. Add them to 1 quart (960ml) of water to soak overnight. Strain the berries, add ice, and sip. (Sumac berries can also be added to boiling water, but the heat lowers the vitamin C content, so iced tea is more nutritious.)

STRAWBERRY

(*Fragaria* × *ananassa*)

■ ZONES: 4 TO 9

It's believed that strawberries were so named because the plants are mulched with straw during the winter, but the exact origin of the name of these sweet berries is unknown. Described as one of America's

most beloved fruits, strawberries are not fruits at all; the edible part of the plant is a receptacle of the flower.

Regardless of the botanical definition, strawberries taste wonderful eaten straight from the vine, baked, or brewed to make flavorful hot or iced tea. The plants are medicinal, too. Strawberries are helpful for stroke and heart disease prevention, blood pressure control, constipation, and blood sugar control; the fruits are chock full of vitamin C, fiber, folic acid, and potassium.

There are more than 600 kinds of strawberries. 'Honeoye' is a June-bearing strawberry that grows 6 inches (15cm) tall and spreads twice as wide when grown in full sun and fertile, moist soil. It produces petite white flowers with yellow centers that bloom in May and June, followed by a single crop of large, sweet berries.

Strawberries can succumb to a number of pests and diseases, making them difficult to grow. Leaf spot, root rot, leather rot, mites, aphids, and slugs are among the most common problems affecting the plants.

In Your Glass:

Strawberries are versatile and can be found in all manner of beverages, including water, lemonade, smoothies, cocktails, and iced tea. The sweet fruits taste great on their own but can also be mixed with banana, coriander, chocolate, vanilla, and nuts. Make a virgin (alcohol-free) strawberry margarita by blending 3 cups (720ml) of strawberries with ½ cup (120ml) of orange juice, ½ cup (120ml) of club soda or sparkling water, 2 tablespoons (30ml) of lime juice, and 2 cups (480ml) of ice. Blend all ingredients on high until it reaches a slushy consistency; pour into margarita glasses (salted rims optional) and garnish with mint leaves.

TOMATO
(*Solanum lycopersicum*)
■ **ZONES:** 3 TO 11

Tomatoes were once thought to be poisonous. In Europe, tomatoes were called poison apples because the fruits, when served on lead-based plates, soaked up the lead, causing illness and death from lead poisoning. As a result, tomatoes were grown as ornamental plants until the 1800s.

The once-shunned fruit is now a popular edible. Tomatoes are classified into two categories: determinate and indeterminate. Determinate tomatoes grow to a determined height, often in the 2- to 4-foot (0.6 to 1.2m) range, and are well-suited to growing in containers. Thanks to their compact size, determinate tomato cultivars, including 'Early Girl,' 'Amelia,' and 'Celebrity,' flower and set fruit quickly. Indeterminate tomatoes do not stop growing when they reach a certain size; some cultivars, such as 'Black Cherry' and

'Creole,' can grow up to 8 feet (2.4m) tall. These extra-tall tomatoes need more room to grow and often require stakes or cages to keep them from falling over.

Heirloom cultivars, such as 'Cherokee Purple,' 'Atkinson,' and 'Arkansas Traveler,' are an alternative to hybrid cultivars and often have richer flavor; some cultivars, including 'Golden Jubilee' and 'Yellow Pear,' produce fruits that are purple, yellow, or multicolored. Tomatoes also come in several sizes and shapes, from cherry (grape) tomatoes to pear-shaped tomatoes.

Grow tomatoes in full sun and in moist, fertile, and well-drained soil. The plants are susceptible to a host of pests and diseases, including tomato hornworms, aphids, cutworms, whiteflies, bacterial spot, blossom-end rot, verticillium wilt, and late blight.

In Your Glass:

So-called seedless cultivars, such as 'Sweet Seedless' and 'Gold Nugget,' contain very few seeds and can be blended into juice or added to tomato juice, mimosas, sangria, and margaritas. Make homemade tomato juice with 1 pound (1.8kg) of chopped, ripe tomatoes, 1 cup (240ml) of chopped celery, ¼ cup (60ml) of chopped onion, 2 tablespoons (30ml) of sugar, some salt, and Tabasco sauce to taste. On the stovetop, bring all ingredients to a simmer and cook, uncovered, until the ingredients are reduced to liquid. Let cool, strain, and refrigerate before serving. Tomatoes pair well with basil, strawberries, watermelon, and even bacon (which can be featured in cocktails!).

Roots

BURDOCK

(*Arctium lappa*)

■ **ZONES:** 3 TO 7

Burdock root is a staple in Asian cooking, where it is often sautéed, braised, and served as a side dish. In the United States, it's often seen as a weed. The root of this exotic herb is packed with antioxidants, increases circulation, alleviates skin conditions like acne and psoriasis, and might inhibit tumor growth. In animal studies, burdock root appears to have aphrodisiac effects. It's also a diuretic and should be taken with care.

Although burdock often grows in natural areas, wild burdock should not be harvested. The plant looks like belladonna nightshade plants, which are toxic. Before consuming burdock root, confirm its source; purchase plants and seeds to plant in a tea garden from a reputable retailer.

Grow burdock in shade and alkaline soil. It produces a large taproot, which you can

use after the first season, but you cannot harvest the seeds of the biennial until the second season. Use dried burdock root to make tea. Dig out the taproot with a shovel—avoid pulling the plant, because the root will break—and then scrub the roots and allow them to dry, which could take several days. Dried roots will be crisp and pliable. You can also dry burdock root in a food dehydrator.

 *In Your Glass:*

Burdock tea is an ancient brew. Add 1 teaspoon (5ml) of dried, chopped burdock root to 2 cups (480ml) of boiling water and steep for fifteen minutes. Strain the roots before drinking. The root has a strong earthy flavor that is best brewed with honey or stevia to improve the taste. Limit consumption of burdock root tea to one cup per day, because it's a diuretic.

CHICORY
(*Cichorium intybus*)

■ **ZONES:** 3 TO 8

Chicory might be best known as a caffeine-free alternative to coffee, but you can also use the roots to make tea. The showy perennial is native to Europe, Asia, and Africa and often considered a weed in the United States (it's listed as an invasive species in Colorado and New Mexico). A taproot that grows beneath the surface of the soil, chicory spreads quickly. Harvest it in the fall, before the first frost.

Despite being a fibrous—and fiber-rich—root, chicory has a creamy flavor. The creaminess pairs well with spices like nutmeg, cinnamon, and cloves.

Chicory grows up to 4 feet (1.2m) tall and 2 feet (60cm) wide, producing green to russet-colored stems and light blue

In Your Glass:

Coffee and tea are natural choices, but chicory has also been used in liqueurs; it adds a rich, bitter component that helps to balance floral notes in a cocktail. To make chicory coffee, grind the root into a fine powder and brew just like conventional coffee. Chicory can also be substituted in most common coffee-based drinks, making it a popular brunch cocktail option.

(sometimes white or pink) flowers with daisy-like petals that close in the afternoon. The flowers bloom in May and June and again in September and October. Due to its aggressive nature, chicory tolerates poor conditions, including drought and poor soil, but it does not like hot, humid climates. Harvesting the root kills the plant, so you will need to replant chicory annually.

Studies have linked chicory, also known as succory, to a host of health benefits, from reducing inflammation and improving gut health to easing constipation. Chicory might trigger an allergic reaction in those sensitive to ragweed. It can also lower blood sugar; therefore, those with diabetes should use it with caution.

GINGER
(*Zingiber officinale*)
■ **ZONES:** 9 TO 12

A tropical plant native to South Asia, ginger can be grown in the United States if the conditions are right. The perennial prefers hot, humid conditions. Growing ginger in a container is ideal, so you can transfer the plant indoors to extend the growing season. The plant will die if left outdoors when temperatures drop below 50°F (10°C).

You can start ginger from a root purchased at the supermarket. Cut the root into 1- to 2-inch (2.5 to 5cm) sections; leave them for twenty-four to forty-eight hours (long enough for the ends to form thin scabs). Choose an area with partial to full shade and plant the root about 1 inch (2.5cm) below the surface of the soil. It takes time for a good-sized rhizome (root) to develop, so allow ginger to grow for a full season before harvesting.

Give ginger room to grow. The plants can grow up to 4 feet (1.2m) tall and spread just as wide, so be sure to provide enough space in the garden. As a garden specimen, ginger is unremarkable—it produces oblong leaves on opposite sides of thick stems—but the root of the ancient spice makes a pungent and healing tea.

Revered for its health benefits, ginger has been a staple of alternative medicine for centuries. The pungent powerhouse is used for nausea and morning sickness, muscle aches, motion sickness, indigestion, and viruses such as colds and flu.

 In Your Glass:

Fresh ginger is a pungent addition to limeade, juice, soda, and even water. Use grated ginger in the veggie juice recipe on page 141. Thanks to its medicinal properties, ginger is also a popular tea. Fruits like apples, apricots, and blackberries add sweetness to balance out the pungent flavor.

GINSENG

(*Panax quinquefolius*)

■ **ZONES:** 4 TO 8

Prized among foragers, ginseng is a sought-after root used to lower inflammation, boost mood, support the immune system, increase energy levels, and lower blood sugar. Ginseng is native to the Ozark and Appalachian regions in the eastern United States, but wild populations are endangered—and, in some regions, extinct—because of overharvesting. The roots were being shipped to China, where populations of their native species, *Panax ginseng*, weren't robust enough to meet demand for the medicinal herb.

This popular herb should not be harvested from the wild but grown in the garden instead. The three-stalked perennial grows up to 15 inches (38cm) tall; small greenish-white flowers with a delicate fragrance appear on the stalks in June and July. When the flowers die, clusters of red berries appear.

Ginseng is difficult to grow. It prefers higher elevations and cooler climates. Choose a location in partial to full shade; under tree canopies, similar to its habitat in the wild, is ideal. Provide moist, neutral soil; if the soil is too acidic, ginseng will die.

Be prepared to wait for a cup of ginseng tea. It takes up to ten years for ginseng roots to grow large enough to be harvested. Avoid damaging the roots during harvest.

 *In Your Glass:*

Fresh and dried ginseng roots are often used to make bitters. The light licorice flavor works well with sweeter flavors. In cocktails and mocktails, pair ginseng with peaches, dates, and lemons. To make ginseng tea, add 2 tablespoons (30ml) of fresh ginseng to 1 cup (240ml) of boiling water; let it steep for five minutes and strain the ginseng before serving. Add 1 teaspoon (5ml) of honey to offset the bitterness.

LICORICE
(*Glycyrrhiza glabra*)
■ **ZONES:** 7 TO 10

In Greek, *glykys* means "sweet" and *rhiza* means "root." The licorice flavor in this perennial—sometimes called sweetwood or sweet root—is used to flavor candies and confections and can be brewed into a flavorful tea.

Licorice is a member of the pea and bean families. There are twenty species of licorice; *Glycyrrhiza glabra* is a popular medicinal plant that is used for sore throats, menstrual cramps, and ulcers. Too much licorice root is associated with heart issues and high blood pressure.

The perennial herb is native to Europe, Africa, and Asia. Pairs of leaves grow on opposite sides of long stems, and light blue-purple flowers (similar in appearance to sweet peas) bloom in the summer. It's the underground rhizomes, which grow up to 3 feet (90cm) long, that make this plant special. The roots are reported to be fifty times sweeter than sugar and can be used fresh or dried to make a sweet tea. It can take two years before the root is established enough to be harvested; commercial growers wait up to four years before harvesting.

Grow licorice in sun to part shade. It prefers sandy, slightly alkaline soil. Licorice is easy to grow from seeds or propagated from cuttings.

 *In Your Glass:*

Make a simple syrup with licorice root. It also makes excellent tea. Add 2 teaspoons (10ml) of dried, chopped licorice root to 1 cup (240ml) of water and let steep for three to five minutes. Strain the roots before drinking.

VALERIAN
(*Valeriana officinalis*)
■ **ZONES:** 4 TO 7

Valerian appears to act as a sedative, making it popular as a sleep aid. The herb is also used to treat hot flashes during menopause, depression, stress, headaches, and muscle and joint pain. The calming compounds in the roots are so powerful that valerian is often viewed as an over-the-counter alternative to Valium.

The evergreen scent and flavor in the leaves and roots make it a popular food additive, but it can be perceived as strong. Pairing it with chamomile, lemon, or peppermint-flavored herbs can help mask the bitterness.

The perennial, also known as garden heliotrope, produces scented leaves and roots; white to pale pink flowers start blooming in June. It grows up to 5 feet (1.5m) high and 4 feet (1.2m) wide. Valerian grows best in full sun and damp locations, but it will also tolerate drier soils. Remove

spent flowers to prevent valerian from self-seeding and taking over the garden.

Valerian is prized for the medicinal properties in its roots—and those healing benefits are strongest in the spring and fall. Accessing the root means uprooting the perennial. Dig up the plant, taking care not to harm the roots, and then hang the plant in a dark location until the roots are dried (it can take a few weeks). Once the roots are dried, clip them and store them in a container in a cool, dark place.

 *In Your Glass:*

To make valerian root tea, mix ½ teaspoon (2.5ml) of dried valerian root with 2 cups (480ml) of boiling water and let steep for three minutes. Strain the roots before sipping. Add honey to reduce the bitterness.

GROW YOUR OWN SWEETENER: STEVIA

Stevia (*Stevia rebaudiana*) is a popular plant-based sweetener that makes an excellent addition to a tea garden. Stevia earned the nicknames "sweetleaf" and "sugarleaf" because the leaves are up to 300 times sweeter than cane sugar.

A perennial in zones 10 and 11 (and an annual in zones 9 and lower), stevia is native to South America and has been used to sweeten the local tea, yerba maté, for more than 1,500 years. The first commercial stevia-based sweetener was developed in the 1970s but not approved in the United States until the early 2000s. It's not allowed as a food ingredient; instead, it is labeled as a dietary supplement.

Stevia has long, slender leaves and produces tubular white flowers in July and August. It thrives in warm temperatures and moist, well-drained soil. It prefers full sun but will tolerate part shade.

Though it's sweet, this member of the aster family has no impact on blood sugar or blood pressure. While researchers believe that stevia is safe, provided it is consumed in moderation, some animal studies linked this sweet herb to lowered sperm production and increased risks of infertility and cancer.

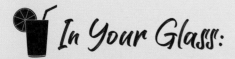 In Your Glass:

Fresh stevia leaves are sweet and can be used plucked right from the plant, but dried leaves are even sweeter. Leaves can also be ground in a food processor to create a fine powder that is used similarly to sugar. Both dried stevia and stevia powder can be stored through the winter.

Chapter 3

MIXING UP THE BEST BEVERAGE GARDEN

You don't have to be a landscape designer (or hire one) to grow a productive and beautiful beverage garden. Choose plants based on their color, fragrance, space and light requirements, or healing properties, and just start experimenting. This chapter includes tips for best practices in cultivating and maintaining your beverage garden, as well as nine suggested garden designs that can be tweaked based on your garden space.

Best Practices

While there are no hard-and-fast rules for planting a beverage garden, following a few best practices will help your garden thrive.

Prepare the soil: Some plants will tolerate poor soil—I'm looking at you, oregano and rosemary—but most prefer a nutrient-rich mix to thrive. Dig down at least 12 inches (30cm) and work in a layer of compost. Rake the soil until it's well mixed and has a loose texture. If soil is compacted, water and oxygen cannot reach the roots. Many plants also prefer well-drained soil because it allows the water to flow through without puddling. Saturated soil can lead to issues such as root rot. Testing the pH of the soil with a kit from the home-improvement store can also provide guidance for soil amendments. For example, acidic soil can burn plants, but adding lime, which is alkaline, can help neutralize the soil.

Assess the location: How much sun does the garden get? Plants that require full sun need at least six hours of sun per day. Too little sun might hamper their growth. On the opposite end of the spectrum, plants

Do not skimp on soil preparation. Be sure to rake your soil.

If necessary, add lime to help neutralize overly acidic soil.

that require partial to full shade might get leaf scald or wither and die if planted in a spot with too much sun. Look at soil drainage, too.

Tend the plants: A little TLC can help small seedlings grow into lush plants that will make countless cocktails, mocktails, smoothies, infused water, and cups of tea. In addition to keeping your garden watered (mornings and evenings when the sun isn't at its peak are the best times), pull weeds to prevent them from choking out the plants, and prune and thin plants as needed.

Watch for pests: If you keep an eye out and spot pests early, you might be able to remove them by hand and simply squish them. Some pests, such as aphids and mites, can be eradicated with a mix of mild

You can test the pH of your own soil with an at-home kit.

Be aware of how much sun each area of your garden will get throughout the year—different plants have different needs.

Pruning plants helps them grow and ultimately helps your harvest.

detergent and water. Mix 2½ tablespoons (37.5ml) of detergent with 1 gallon (3.8 liters) of water, fill a squirt bottle, and spray the leaves. If a more aggressive approach is needed, choose pesticides like neem oil, copper sulfate, and hydrogen peroxide that are approved for use in organic gardens. You'll want to steer clear of harsh chemicals because you'll be using the plants in the beverages you'll be imbibing.

Think about garden structure: Planting directly into a new or existing garden bed is always an option. Often, though, soil quality is poor, so you may need to add amendments like peat moss, manure, grass clippings, and compost to boost soil health. Building a raised bed that you can fill with bags of nutrient-rich organic matter provides a good base for plants. Planting in containers is another good option—just make sure to use potting soil, not garden soil, because garden soil is heavier and can

Water in the mornings and evenings.

Spray aphids and mites with a mix of mild detergent and water.

become compacted, preventing water from reaching the roots. Containers are also a great choice for herbs like mint that spread quickly and can take over the garden if not kept in check.

Avoid overharvesting: It may seem counterintuitive, but it's best to harvest the tender new growth, not the larger, more mature leaves. Young leaves offer the most flavor, and leaving the larger, lower leaves also helps promote vigorous plant growth—but don't pluck too many of those tender leaves. Overharvesting depletes supplies and, in the wild, can make it harder for plants to survive. If you're planning to make big batches of beverages, plant extra herbs and harvest smaller quantities from each.

Raised beds allow you to precisely control the soil base in which your plants grow.

City Living

Just because you live in an apartment or without access to a yard doesn't mean that you can't grow your own beverage ingredients. You may be somewhat more limited by space and light, but you can still grow a ton of different plants that can be used in your favorite drinks, so don't be discouraged. Another option is to join a community garden. Often located at churches and community centers, or in parks, these plots will provide all of the space you need to

Utilize your window space to give your plants the light they need.

get growing. In really dense cities, you'll even find gardens on roofs! Membership fees are usually quite low; plus, you can meet others who share your interests.

A rooftop community garden is a great idea for a city dweller.

Garden Designs

Do you have specific needs or tastes that you want your garden to fulfill? Or do you just like the idea of having a theme? Whatever the case, I've prepared nine different plant layout suggestions for your garden. If you have the space, you could even create all nine of these gardens in different spots.

LEMONADE STAND GARDEN

Lemonade made with just-picked, freshly squeezed juices from lemons (page 78), strawberries (page 85), raspberries (page 80), and peppermint (page 44) tastes so good, you'll be tempted to set up a lemonade stand to share the tart, sweet drinks with the neighbors.

DRINK YOUR VEGGIES GARDEN

Instead of using the tomatoes (page 86), carrots (page 74), beets (page 70), spinach (page 83), and kale (page 77) in this setup for salads, use the fresh veggies to make delicious, nutritious juices.

GARNISH GARDEN

Garden-to-glass beverages should look as good as they taste. Grow lavender (page 65), parsley (page 43), strawberries (page 85), basil (page 37), and lavender mint (page 38) to add a pop of color and style to your favorite drinks (and feel free to eat them while you sip).

LOVELY LEMON GARDEN

Lemon is one of those rare flavors that is both soothing and uplifting. Although this garden is filled with lemony herbs, each one—lemon verbena (page 41), lemon balm (page 39), bee balm (page 29), lemon basil (page 37), and lemon thyme (page 56)— offers a subtly different lemon flavor that you'll love adding to your favorite drinks.

H₂O INFUSIONS GARDEN

You don't need to go to the spa to drink flavored water. Grow cucumbers (page 76), lavender (page 65), basil (page 37), spearmint (page 48), and strawberries (page 85) and add them to your water for refreshing, no-calorie beverages that will quench your thirst and please your palate.

SOOTHING TEA GARDEN

Few things are more soothing than a hot cup of tea, especially when it's made from ingredients you grew. Peppermint (page 44), lavender (page 65), echinacea (page 62), and lemon verbena (page 41) are easy-to-grow herbs that can be turned into simple, flavorful teas—which you can then sweeten with stevia (page 93).

SPEARMINT

PEPPERMINT

APPLE MINT

PINEAPPLE MINT

MINT MEDLEY GARDEN

Mint is easy to grow and adds a punch of flavor to tea, water, lemonade, mint juleps, and mojitos. Grow different varieties, including spearmint (page 48), peppermint (page 44), apple mint (page 27), and pineapple mint (page 27), to experience subtle differences in flavors.

CLASSIC COCKTAILS GARDEN

Skip the store-bought ingredients and grow a garden filled with peppermint (page 44), cucumbers (page 76), blood oranges (page 73), and celery (page 75), which provide the fresh flavors in classic cocktails such as mint juleps, garden gin and tonics, whiskey sours, and Bloody Marys.

ECHINACEA

PURPLE PASSIONFLOWER

CHAMOMILE

CALENDULA

TRUMPET HONEYSUCKLE

EDIBLE FLOWER GARDEN

Some of the prettiest flowers in the garden taste as good as they look. Plant echinacea (page 62), purple passionflower (page 66), chamomile (page 60), calendula (page 59), and trumpet honeysuckle (page 68) to use their petals in teas and other libations.

Chapter 4

FROM CULTIVATION TO CUP: MAKING PERFECT DRINKS

From the tools you use, to the preparation methods you choose, to the way you preserve your plants for future use, masterfully making beverages with ingredients from your garden takes a little know-how. In this chapter, you'll learn everything you need to ensure that each drink you prepare is a symphony of taste. Happy sipping!

Preparation

Brewing a cup of tea can be as simple as steeping a handful of fresh herbs in boiling water; making infused waters requires no more effort than adding combinations of fruits and herbs to cold water; and crafting cocktails and mocktails can be done with big-brand spirits and supermarket mixers. Still, making *great* garden-to-glass beverages requires some preparation. Follow these tips for turning your harvest into truly delicious drinks.

Steer clear of chemicals: Using sustainable methods to grow herbs, flowers, and fruit ensures that your beverage ingredients are free of toxic pesticides and

Don't be tempted to forage for plants like dandelions near high-traffic areas where they could be contaminated by brake dust and other chemicals.

herbicides. Avoid harvesting tea ingredients such as dandelions, chickweed, and red clover in areas that might have been exposed to chemicals. Avoid growing or harvesting herbs near high-traffic areas; brake dust and other chemical residues can be hard to wash off.

Get educated: Not all foods are safe for steeping. Before heading out to the garden to pluck ingredients for garden-to-glass beverages, make sure that the plants are edible—and that you've correctly identified the species. If in doubt, purchase a field guide to help you identify safe plants or take foraging classes to learn

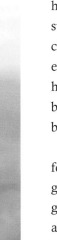

These pokeweed berries look delicious, but they aren't safe to steep (or eat).

No matter how clean you keep your garden, wash everything you harvest before consuming it.

from a knowledgeable mentor. Talking to a naturopath or herbalist about which herbs might interact negatively with medications or health conditions is also a good idea.

Wash everything: Thoroughly wash all foods plucked from the garden before using them in culinary drink recipes.

Follow local laws: Foraging for wild foods can be a great way to supplement the ingredients growing in your garden, but remember that harvesting wild foods is illegal in some areas, including national parks. Check your local laws before you pluck.

Clean the equipment: Be sure to wash all of your equipment, including pans, drying racks, food dehydrators, teapots, tea-ball strainers, cocktail shakers, blenders, and mortars and pestles, thoroughly between uses. Cleaning the equipment not only eradicates bacteria but also ensures that the flavors won't transfer between recipes, so you will get the pure tastes you want.

Store safely: Store dried herbs in airtight containers in a dark space (like a cupboard) for up to one year. See page 119 for more information on drying your plants before storage.

ESSENTIAL TOOLS FOR GARDEN-TO-GLASS DRINKS

You don't need fancy equipment to make mocktails, cocktails, teas, and infusions, but there are some tools that can make it easier to turn your harvest into delicious drinks.

Blender or juicer: If you plan to make smoothies or juices, invest in decent equipment to quickly and thoroughly blend all of the ingredients.

Juice press: Skip the "slice and squeeze" and get the juice from lemons, limes, and other citrus fruits with a juice press. The gadget allows you to get more juice than you can with a powerful squeeze.

French press: The plunger in this tool pushes the tea leaves to the bottom and the piping hot brew to the top—no straining required.

Kettle: Sure, you can boil water in a saucepan, but a kettle, whether an electric or stovetop model, has a lid and spout perfect for pouring hot water into a cup or teapot.

Measuring cups: Experiment with different amounts of ingredients (both on their own and in blends) and take notes on which measurements lead to the perfect beverages. In cocktail speak, measuring cups for liquids are called "jiggers" (shown) and have a unique hourglass-style design.

Mortar and pestle: These old-fashioned tools are ideal for crumbling dried leaves to make loose-leaf teas and tea blends or to muddle ingredients for cocktails. A muddler (shown), which has a handle and a flat end, is another option.

Shakers: Mixing ingredients can get messy. The two halves of a Boston shaker look like pint glasses and fit together to allow you to seamlessly mix several different ingredients.

Sieve: For larger batches of loose-leaf tea, a sieve is essential to separate the leaves from the steeped tea. Similar to a sieve, a mesh strainer sits on top of a glass and strains out excess ingredients like herbs and fruit that you don't want mixing with the liquid of your cocktails and mocktails.

Tea-ball strainer: Filling a tea-ball strainer with loose-leaf tea is a good way to avoid straining leaves before drinking tea. They come in many shapes. For multiple batches, you could also package tea like the pros with tea filter bags. Look for unbleached options; the models with drawstrings are the easiest to use.

WHAT'S IN A GLASS?

The size and shape of the glass you choose for your favorite cocktails impacts the scent and flavor of your drink. Stock your bar with these six must-have glasses to ensure that you have the right vessel for every garden-to-glass cocktail you mix.

Champagne flute: No bubbly? No problem. Champagne flutes are not just for champagne; these slender glasses are also designed to preserve the bubbles in drinks such as mimosas, Bellinis, and French 75s, plus any sparkling mocktails.

Coupe: A rounded version of the conical-shaped martini glass, the coupe is the right glass to use for cocktails that are shaken or stirred and served chilled, no ice.

Highball: This tall, skinny glass is a go-to behind the bar. You should use highball glasses for basic mixed drinks like vodka and sodas, gin and tonics, and whiskey and gingers. The Collins glass, a tall (but not necessarily skinny) glass, can also be used in place of a highball glass, but be warned: Collins glasses have room for a few extra ounces, which could lead you to drink more alcohol or add too much mixer, watering down your drink.

Margarita: A margarita glass is used mostly for margaritas, but the oversized glass is nice to have on hand for extra-large cocktails. Drinks normally served in a coupe glass could also be served in a margarita glass.

Martini: Martini glasses are not just for martinis. The conical-shaped glasses are used for cocktails between 3 and 6 ounces (90 and 180ml) that are served without ice. Brandy Alexanders, Manhattans, and cosmopolitans are all served in martini glasses.

Rocks: As the name suggests, rocks glasses are used for spirits served on the rocks. Single rocks glasses hold 8 to 10 ounces (240 to 300ml), while double rocks glasses (also called double old fashioned glasses) can accommodate up to 12 ounces (355ml). Double rocks glasses are used for cocktails with ice like old fashioneds, Negronis, white Russians, and Palomas.

The Best Tea Brews

Depending on the type of tea you are brewing, you will want to hit a particular water temperature, use a set quantity of tea, and steep for a specific length of time. This will unlock the best, purest flavors of the tea.

TYPE OF TEA	WATER TEMPERATURE	QUANTITY	STEEP TIME
White	160–185°F (71–85°C)	1 tablespoon (15ml) of tea per cup (240ml) of water	2–3 minutes
Green	170–185°F (77–85°C)	1 teaspoon (5ml) of tea per cup (240ml) of water	3–5 minutes
Oolong	185–205°F (85–96°C)	1 teaspoon (5ml) of tea per cup (240ml) of water	1–3 minutes
Black	190–205°F (88–96°C)	1 teaspoon (5ml) of tea per cup (240ml) of water	3–5 minutes
Tisane	Any temperature	Depends on herbs	To taste

When stored properly, dried herbs are safe from bacteria and mold.

Preserving the Harvest

You could stick to making drinks solely from fresh herbs, but learning how to dry them allows you to preserve the harvest and make garden-to-glass beverages all year long. Dried herbs are also safe from bacteria and mold and retain their flavor and potency for up to one year. For the best results, use one of the following three methods for drying herbs. For each, always wash herbs first and then pat them dry with a clean paper towel to remove as much moisture as possible. Once the herbs have dried, store them in glass jars with lids, and label the jars with the herb (or blend) and the date.

Air-drying: This low-tech method has worked for centuries. Harvest a bundle of herbs; tie the stems together with a twist tie; wrap the bundle with a mesh or muslin bag that is thin enough to allow air circulation while catching any falling leaves; and hang the bundle upside down. You can also place

Glass jars are a good option when storing teas.

Air-drying is a classic and almost foolproof method of preserving your harvest.

Make your oven into an herb dryer.

Using a food dehydrator can be an efficient way to dry herbs.

herbs on a drying screen (an old, clean window screen is a good DIY option). Simply place a muslin cloth over the screen, line the screen with a single layer of herbs, and leave the herbs to dry. Depending on the moisture content, herbs can take several hours or several days to dry. Herbs are dried when they crumble easily.

Oven-drying: Choose the lowest heat setting possible—less than 180°F (82°C) is ideal, because if the temperature is too high, the herbs will bake, not dry. Place a single layer of herbs on a cookie sheet and place it in the oven. Leave the oven door open a crack to allow air to circulate. Check the herbs every fifteen minutes. Low-moisture herbs, such as oregano, marjoram, and rosemary, will require less time than other herbs that have higher moisture content. Expect oven-drying herbs to take at least forty-five minutes; some will take much longer. Let herbs cool before handling them.

Dehydrating: Food dehydrators are excellent for drying herbs. While it's best to follow the instructions in the operating manual, as a general rule of thumb, preheat the dehydrator to 115°F (46°C) (higher if you live in a humid climate). Place herbs on trays in a single layer, making note of which herbs are on which trays; it can be hard to tell dried herbs apart. Set the timer. Expect it to take at least one hour—but potentially much longer—for the herbs to fully dry. Check them every fifteen minutes to monitor their progress. After you remove the herbs from the dehydrator, allow them to cool before handling.

Three Tips for Great Culinary Beverages

Morning is the best time to harvest herbs.

Harvest early: To seal in the flavor, cut herbs first thing in the morning. Use a sharp pair of shears to clip the leaves after the dew has dried but before the sun gets too hot; the heat draws out the natural oils that give herbs their flavor. Instead of letting herbs grow wild, harvest them often. Snipping a few sprigs or a handful of leaves serves as an informal pruning. Harvesting herbs before they start to flower keeps the energy in the leaves, which helps preserve their fresh flavors.

Air-drying herbs is a natural way to preserve their maximum flavor.

Dry herbs naturally: You can keep sipping the flavors of your labor all winter long by drying fresh herbs harvested in the summer. Lay the leaves on a towel in the hot sun until they turn crispy. The leaves must be dry enough to crumble; if there is any moisture left in them, they will get moldy. Once the leaves are dried, store them in glass jars in a cool, dry place.

Don't be afraid to mix different teas and herbs together. You might hit upon a real winner!

Have fun: Growing the ingredients for your beverages is all about experimentation. Start with a few favorites; sample new plants; mix and match like a mad scientist and see what happens. Not all DIY blends will be a hit, but some flavor combinations might lead to surprisingly tasty drinks.

Chapter 5

SHAKEN, NOT STIRRED: RECIPES FOR THE PERFECT GARDEN-TO-GLASS BEVERAGES

In this chapter, you'll learn about simple syrups and shrubs, which are the building blocks for cocktails and mocktails, and find inspiration (and recipes) for a wide variety of delicious drinks, both alcoholic and alcohol-free, that will intrigue your taste buds while making good use of your garden. After you've mixed a few drinks you love, try experimenting with individual ingredients to develop new drinks and use every bit of your harvest. The possibilities are truly endless.

All text and recipes for simple syrups, shrubs (except for Two-Stage Shrub), and alcoholic drinks are courtesy Jeanette Hurt, author of *Drink Like a Woman*.

Experiment with different sugars and infusions for your simple syrups, like this basil one.

Simple Syrups

A simple syrup consists of equal parts sugar and hot water and is a basic building block for cocktails and mocktails. When you switch out granulated sugar for honey or flavor the syrup with herbs, fruits, or vegetables, magic happens. **All recipes make roughly 2 cups (480ml) of simple syrup.**

BASIC SIMPLE SYRUP

Heat sugar and water over high heat, stirring constantly until sugar is completely dissolved. To sweeten basic simple syrup, add additional sugar or switch out granulated sugar for brown sugar, turbinado sugar, honey, or maple syrup. Cool to room temperature before use. Store in the refrigerator for up to two weeks; simple syrup can be frozen for up to six months.

- 2 cups (480ml) water
- 2 cups (480ml) granulated sugar

MINT SIMPLE SYRUP

Heat sugar and water over high heat, stirring constantly until sugar is completely dissolved. Remove from heat, add mint leaves, stir, and cover; let sit at room temperature for two hours. Strain mint leaves before use. You can also replace mint with basil, lemon verbena, chamomile, sage, or any other herbs growing in your garden.

- 2 cups (480ml) water
- 2 cups (480ml) granulated sugar
- 1 cup (240ml) packed mint leaves

LAVENDER SIMPLE SYRUP

Heat sugar and water over high heat, stirring constantly until sugar is completely dissolved. Stir in the lavender blossoms, remove from heat, cover, and let sit at room temperature for two hours. Strain the blossoms away before use.

- 2 cups (480ml) water
- 2 cups (480ml) granulated sugar
- 1 cup (240ml) fresh lavender blossoms or ½ cup (120ml) dried lavender blossoms

RHUBARB SIMPLE SYRUP

Heat sugar and water over high heat, stirring constantly until sugar is completely dissolved. Add the rhubarb chunks, reduce heat to medium, and let simmer for about five minutes. Remove from heat and let cool. Once cooled, strain the liquid and discard the solids.

- 2 cups (480ml) water
- 2 cups (480ml) granulated sugar
- 4 pounds (1.8kg) fresh rhubarb, cut into chunks

HIBISCUS SIMPLE SYRUP

In a medium-sized pot, bring all ingredients to a boil over medium-high heat. Turn off heat and allow to cool and steep at room temperature for two or more hours. Strain, then chill.

- 2 cups (480ml) water
- 2 cups (480ml) granulated sugar
- 4 cups (960ml) fresh hibiscus flowers or 2 cups (480ml) dried hibiscus flowers

Shrubs

A shrub is basically equal parts sugar, fruit, and vinegar, and it is a concoction that is used mixed with spirits, sparkling wine, beer, and sparkling water. Shrubs can be made with any kind of fruit, sweetener, or vinegar; apple cider and wine or champagne vinegars are the best choices to add a hint of acidity and sourness. Enjoy experimenting with different combinations. **All recipes make roughly 1 cup (240ml) of shrub;** multiply the quantities to scale up the production if you like the recipe or have a lot of fruit to use up before it goes bad.

This gin, blackberry shrub, and thyme cocktail has a nice, fresh bite.

A Word on Mocktails

Skip the ice in a mocktail.

A well-made mocktail has all of the taste, elegance, and feel of a real cocktail without the alcohol. Experiment with combining shrubs, simple syrups, fresh juices, and tonics to make delicious concoctions that will rival regular cocktails. For a gin-like mocktail, make a simple syrup of juniper berries (use the lavender simple syrup recipe on page 125 and substitute juniper berries), and then combine it with juices and tonics. Make sure all of your ingredients are chilled, and serve mocktails with little to no ice, because, while ice and water release the aromas of booze, both water down mocktails.

—Jeanette Hurt

A Basic Primer on Bitters

Many of the cocktail recipes in the following pages include bitters. Bitters, which are high-proof spirits that are infused with fruits, bark, roots, and herbs, are the spices of the cocktail world. Rather than making your own, purchase bitters from local liquor stores or search online for small-batch bitters from companies like Crude Bitters and Copper & Kings. When using bitters, less is more: a dash or two will enhance your cocktails and balance out the other flavors.

—Jeanette Hurt

Just a small quantity of bitters goes a long way.

BASIC SHRUB

Chop up fruit. Stir fruit and sugar together until incorporated (fully mixed), then stir in vinegar, cover, and let sit for twenty-four to forty-eight hours in the refrigerator. Strain the liquid and discard the solids.

- 1 cup (240ml) fruit
- 1 cup (240ml) sugar
- 1 cup (240ml) vinegar

HOT-PROCESS SHRUB

Chop up fruit. Stir fruit and sugar together until incorporated, then stir in vinegar. Bring the mixture to a boil, then reduce to a simmer and let cook on low or medium-low heat for ten to fifteen minutes or until the fruit starts falling apart. Let cool completely, strain the liquid, and discard the solids.

- 2 cups (480ml) fruit
- 1 cup (240ml) sugar
- 1 cup (240ml) vinegar

TWO-STAGE SHRUB

This method requires a little more time but allows you to eat the fruit afterward. Chop up fruit. Stir fruit and sugar together until incorporated, cover, and let sit for twenty-four to forty-eight hours in the refrigerator. Strain the liquid and set aside the sugary solids to snack on or use in desserts. Mix the strained liquid with the vinegar, cover, and let sit for another twenty-four hours in the refrigerator.

- 1 cup (240ml) fruit
- 1 cup (240ml) sugar
- 1 cup (240ml) vinegar

Cocktails

All cocktail recipes make one cocktail unless otherwise noted.

HIBISCUS FRENCH 75

Floral yet herbaceous, this is a refreshing and sophisticated cocktail.

Shake all ingredients except sparkling wine together for about sixty seconds. Strain into flute, top with sparkling wine, and garnish. For a variation, swap the hibiscus simple syrup with lavender simple syrup.

- 1½ ounces (45ml) gin with floral aromas
- ¾ ounce (22ml) fresh lemon juice
- ¾ ounce (22ml) hibiscus simple syrup (page 125)
- dash of citrus bitters
- 2 to 3 ounces (60 to 90ml) sparkling wine or champagne
- glass: champagne flute
- garnish: fresh hibiscus and/or lemon peel

GARDEN WHISKEY SOUR WITH EGG WHITE

A fresh twist on a popular classic cocktail, this botanical beverage makes good use of the herbs growing in your garden.

Makes 2 servings.

In a dry shaker, add the egg white. Shake for one minute with nothing else added. Then add the whiskey, lemon juice, and simple syrup. Shake for two more minutes without ice. Pour into a glass. Place half of the herbs into the bottom of the shaker. Use a muddler to press them in a clockwise motion, three to four times, to express their oils. Add the cocktail, fill with ice, and then shake vigorously for two to three minutes until foamy. Add the remaining herbs. Shake for one more minute, then strain into two cocktail glasses filled with ice or into chilled coupe glasses without ice. Add garnishes.

- 1 egg white
- 3 ounces (90ml) whiskey
- 1½ ounces (45ml) freshly squeezed lemon juice
- 1½ ounces (45ml) simple syrup (page 124) (or use an herbal simple syrup)
- 6 to 10 leaves of your choice of herb like lemon verbena, pineapple sage, thyme (if using thyme, use about 1 teaspoon [5ml] leaves), savory, etc.
- dash of citrus bitters
- glass: rocks or Collins with ice or coupe without ice
- garnish: sprigs of herbs and lemon wheels or wedges

RHUBARB GIMLET

This is a summery, tangy twist on a gimlet.

Shake all ingredients together with ice for sixty seconds. Strain into rocks glass filled with ice. Add garnish.

- 1½ ounces (45ml) gin or vodka
- ¾ ounce (22ml) lime juice
- ¾ ounce (22ml) rhubarb simple syrup (page 125)
- dash of citrus bitters
- glass: rocks
- garnish: sprig of basil

GARDEN MARGARITA WITH STRAWBERRIES AND BASIL

Nothing says summer like a fruit-forward margarita, and if you grow fresh basil, then this is the cocktail for you.

Place all ingredients into a blender. Blend on high until slushy. Pour into glass and add garnish.

- 1½ ounces (45ml) blanco tequila

- ¾ ounce (22ml) orange liqucur

- ¾ ounce (22ml) basil simple syrup (use the mint simple syrup recipe on page 125, but swap the mint with basil; cinnamon Thai basil works really well with this cocktail)

- ¾ ounce (22ml) fresh lime juice

- 3 to 5 fresh strawberries

- ½ cup (120ml) ice cubes

- glass: margarita or martini

- garnish: fresh strawberry and fresh basil

MINT JULEP

Use freshly harvested herbs to mix this cocktail to celebrate the Kentucky Derby.

Place all ingredients into a shaker filled with ice. Shake hard for about thirty to sixty seconds. Pour the mixture into a julep or rocks glass filled with crushed ice. Garnish with mint sprig.

- 2 ounces (60ml) bourbon
- 1½ ounces (45ml) mint simple syrup (see page 125; preferably made with 'Kentucky Colonel' mint, which was cultivated for the julep, or another type of spearmint, but any mint can be used)
- ½ ounce (15ml) water
- 4 to 6 mint leaves
- dash of citrus bitters
- glass: julep or rocks
- garnish: mint sprig

MOJITO

Nothing says summer on the patio like a freshly made mojito with mint grown in your garden.

Place mint leaves, syrup, lime juice, and citrus bitters into the bottom of a shaker. Gently press a few times with a muddler, fill with ice, and add rum. Shake for about thirty seconds. Strain into highball or Collins glass filled with ice, then top with seltzer or club soda. Gently slap the mint sprig before adding it to the glass with the lime wheel or wedge.

- 1½ ounces (45ml) white rum
- ¾ ounce (22ml) mint simple syrup (page 125)
- ¾ ounce (22ml) fresh lime juice
- 4 to 6 mint leaves
- dash of citrus bitters
- 3 to 4 ounces (90 to 120ml) seltzer or club soda
- glass: highball or Collins
- garnish: mint sprig and lime wheel or wedge

LAVENDER MOJITO

Fresh lavender makes this variation a little bit sweeter than the original mojito, but it's equally refreshing on a hot summer day.

Place mint leaves, syrups (only ¼ ounce [7.5ml] lavender syrup), lime juice, and bitters into the bottom of a shaker. Gently press a few times with a muddler, fill with ice, and add rum. Shake for about thirty seconds. Strain into highball or Collins glass filled with ice, then top with seltzer or club soda. Drizzle remaining ½ ounce (15ml) lavender syrup into the mojito. Gently slap the mint sprig before adding it to the glass with the lime wheel or wedge.

- 1½ ounces (45ml) white rum
- ¾ ounce (22ml) mint simple syrup (page 125)
- ¼ ounce (7.5ml) lavender simple syrup and ½ ounce (15ml) lavender simple syrup, separated (page 125)
- ¾ ounce (22ml) fresh lime juice
- 4 to 6 mint leaves
- dash of citrus bitters and/or lavender bitters
- 3 to 4 ounces (90 to 120ml) seltzer or club soda
- glass: highball or Collins
- garnish: mint sprig and lime wheel or wedge

RED SANGRIA

Sangria is the ultimate party punch. Fruit, sugar, and spirits meld with a bottle of red wine.

Makes 8 servings.

Into a large carafe or pitcher, stir sugar, fruit, and bitters together. Let sit for about five to ten minutes to let the fruits and bitters melt into the sugar. Stir in orange liqueur, brandy, and red wine. Taste to see if it is sweetened to your liking. If it's not sweet enough, add more sugar by the tablespoon. Serve over ice with extra slices of fruit or refrigerate until ready to use, but not for longer than six to eight hours. For endless variations, you can change the fruit and wine. Use white wines and fresh peaches, apricots, or berries for a white sangria; use a rosé wine and pink berries or cherries to make a blush sangria; and sparkling wine and berries make the perfect sparkling sangria.

- ¼ cup (60ml) sugar
- 1 orange, thinly sliced
- 1 lemon, thinly sliced
- 1 lime, thinly sliced
- 1 apple, thinly sliced
- 4 dashes of Angostura or old fashioned bitters
- 1 bottle red wine
- ¼ cup (60ml) orange liqueur
- ¼ cup (60ml) brandy
- glass: pitcher and stemless red wine glasses
- garnish: mint leaves

WHISKEY AND PEACHES

This is a garden-fresh riff on a Southern Comfort Manhattan, but there's no SoCo in this recipe.

Stir all ingredients together for about sixty seconds or until chilled. Strain into rocks glass filled with ice or chilled coupe or martini glass. Garnish with a slice of peach.

- 1½ ounces (45ml) bourbon or rye whiskey
- ½ ounce (15ml) red vermouth
- ½ ounce (15ml) peach shrub (page 127)
- ½ ounce (15ml) peach liqueur
- 2 dashes of Angostura or old fashioned bitters
- glass: rocks if serving with ice, coupe or martini if serving without
- garnish: peach slice

- 1½ to 2 ounces (45 to 60ml) gin, especially an herbaceous or floral gin

- ¾ ounce (22ml) lime juice

- 3 to 4 ounces (90 to 120ml) tonic water

- 1 to 2 tablespoons (15 to 30ml) herbs, dried juniper berries, slices of cucumbers, ripe berries, etc.— whatever herbs match the profile of the gin you are using

- glass: goblet or double rocks

- garnish: besides the herbs and berries, add a wheel or wedge of lime to the glass

GARDEN G AND T

In Spain, gin and tonics are served in goblets filled with ice, gin and tonic, and juniper berries and other aromatics that are found in the gin or emphasized by the tonic. You can add edible flowers, herbs, and other just-harvested items from your garden.

Fill a shaker with ice, pour in gin and lime juice, and stir for about thirty seconds to chill. Pour into glass filled with ice, then top with tonic water and herb mixture. Garnish with a wheel or wedge of lime.

Alcohol-Free Drinks

MMM MINT ICED TEA

Hot or iced, mint tea is nice, and these three mint varieties, each with their own distinct flavor, blend perfectly in a tangy but not-too-sweet cup of tea.

Makes 3 to 4 servings.

Boil the water, add the leaves to the water, and leave to steep in the refrigerator overnight. Strain the leaves, pour the water over ice, and sip. You can also enjoy this tea hot by boiling the water, adding the ingredients, and steeping for ten minutes. Strain the leaves, pour into a warm mug, and serve.

- 1 teaspoon (5ml) fresh spearmint leaves
- 1 teaspoon (5ml) fresh peppermint leaves
- 1 teaspoon (5ml) fresh lavender mint leaves
- 4 cups (960ml) water

CITRUS LIFT TEA

Need a pick-me-up? The distinct citrus flavors in these popular herbs blend perfectly for an uplifting (and aromatic) cup of tea.

Makes 3 to 4 servings.

Boil the water; add the lemon verbena, lemon balm, and bee balm; and steep for three to five minutes. Strain the leaves, pour the tea into a warm mug, and serve.

- 1 tablespoon (15ml) fresh lemon verbena leaves

- 1 tablespoon (15ml) fresh lemon balm leaves

- 1 tablespoon (15ml) fresh bee balm leaves

- 4 cups (960ml) water

LAVENDER LEMONADE

This upmarket twist on traditional lemonade looks as good as it tastes. **Makes 8 servings.**

Boil water, add sugar, and simmer on low heat for five to seven minutes, stirring often. When the sugar is dissolved, remove from heat and add lemon juice and lavender. Let the lemonade cool to room temperature, remove the lavender sprigs, and refrigerate overnight.

- 8 cups (1.9L) water
- 1 cup (240ml) sugar
- 1½ cups (360ml) juice from a Meyer lemon
- 10 sprigs fresh lavender

VEGGIE JUICE

Skip the juice bar and make fresh juice from the vegetables in your garden.

Makes 2 servings.

Wash, peel, and chop all vegetables and fruit into small chunks. Add to the juicer and blend until smooth. Add the lemon juice and grated ginger and refrigerate for at least one hour. Serve over ice. If the lemon juice doesn't add enough sweetness, add more to taste.

- 2 large beets
- 5 carrots
- 2 apples
- juice from 1 Meyer lemon
- 1 tablespoon (15ml) grated ginger

FRUIT SMOOTHIE

A fruit smoothie is like a milkshake for grown-ups. Unlike simple fruit juice, which is stripped of its fiber and often manufactured with added sugar, homemade fruit smoothies maintain all of their nutrients.

Makes 5 servings.

Put all ingredients in a blender and mix until smooth. Pour into glasses and serve.

- 2 cups (480ml) strawberries
- 1 banana
- 1 cup (240ml) almond milk
- ½ cup (120ml) plain yogurt
- 1 tablespoon (15ml) peanut butter
- 1 cup (240ml) ice

INFUSED WATER

Trade boring bottled water for a fruit- and vegetable-infused version that is sure to quench your thirst.

Makes 8 servings.

Add fruit, herbs, and water to a pitcher. Refrigerate overnight. Remove basil and lemon slices (and strawberries, if desired). Pour over ice and serve.

- 1 cup (240ml) strawberries, sliced
- 10 large basil leaves, chopped into large pieces
- 2 Meyer lemons, thinly sliced
- 8 cups (1.9L) of water

PLANT HARDINESS ZONE MAPS

The United States map shown here is a modified reproduction of the official USDA Plant Hardiness Zone Map. To view the official map, which includes the "a" and "b" subzones, go to *https://planthardiness.ars.usda.gov*.

AVERAGE ANNUAL EXTREME MINIMUM TEMPERATURE
1976–2005

TEMP (°F)	ZONE	TEMP (°C)
-60 to -50	1	-51.1 to -45.6
-50 to -40	2	-45.6 to -40
-40 to -30	3	-40 to -34.4
-30 to -20	4	-34.4 to -28.9
-20 to -10	5	-28.9 to -23.3
-10 to 0	6	-23.3 to -17.8
0 to 10	7	-17.8 to -12.2
10 to 20	8	-12.2 to -6.7
20 to 30	9	-6.7 to -1.1
30 to 40	10	-1.1 to 4.4
40 to 50	11	4.4 to 10
50 to 60	12	10 to 15.6
60 to 70	13	15.6 to 21.1

UNITED STATES

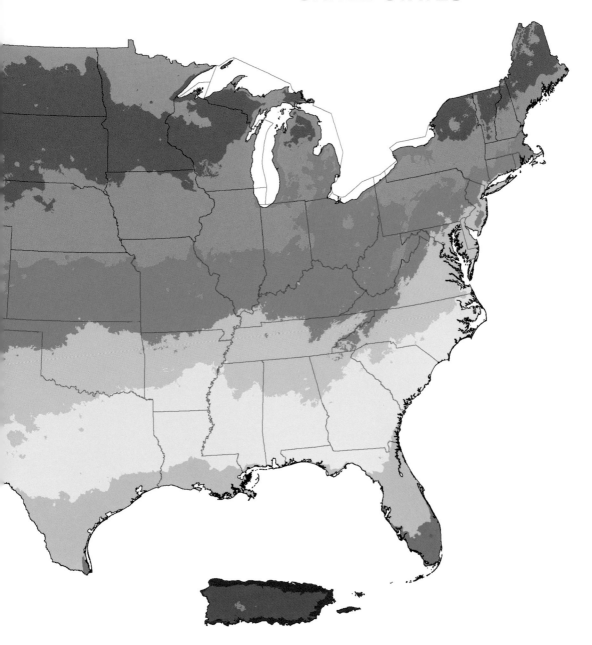

From the United States Department of Agriculture (USDA) website, *www.planthardiness.ars.usda.gov.*

EXTREME MINIMUM TEMPERATURE ZONES

TEMP (°F)	ZONE	TEMP (°C)
-70 to -65	0a	-56.7 to -53.9
-65 to -60	0b	-53.9 to -51.1
-60 to -55	1a	-51.1 to -48.3
-55 to -50	1b	-48.3 to -45.6
-50 to -45	2a	-45.6 to -42.8
-45 to -40	2b	-42.8 to -40.0
-40 to -35	3a	-40.0 to -37.2
-35 to -30	3b	-37.2 to -34.3
-30 to -25	4a	-34.3 to -31.7
-25 to -20	4b	-31.7 to -28.9
-20 to -15	5a	-28.9 to -26.1
-15 to -10	5b	-26.1 to -23.3
-10 to -5	6a	-23.3 to -20.6
-5 to 0	6b	-20.6 to -17.8
0 to 5	7a	-17.8 to -15.0
5 to 10		-15.0 to -12.2
10 to 15		-12.2 to -9.4
15 to 20	8b	-9.4 to -6.7
20 to 25	9a	-6.7 to -3.9

CANADA

Resolute

mbridge Bay

N U N A V U T

IQALUIT

NEWFOUNDLAND AND LABRADOR

Rankin Inlet

Kuujjuaq

Churchill

Happy Valley-
Goose Bay

ST JOHN'S

Chisasibi

QUÉBEC

ANITOBA

PEI
ÎLE-P-É

CHARLOTTETOWN

N B
N-B

FREDERICTON

NIPEG
randon

ONTARIO

QUÉBEC

HALIFAX

NOVA SCOTIA

Kenora

Thunder
Bay

Sault
Ste Marie

Montréal

OTTAWA

TORONTO

From Natural Resources Canada website,
www.planthardiness.gc.ca

RESOURCES

AMERICAN MEADOWS

877-309-7333

www.americanmeadows.com

A Vermont-based online retailer that has been supplying gardeners with high-quality seeds and perennials for more than thirty years.

CAMELLIA FOREST NURSERY

919-968-0504

www.camforest.com

Offers an incredible selection of *Camellia* varieties, including several varieties of *Camellia sinensis*. Ships seeds or mature plants nationwide. The North Carolina nursery offers tours of its tea gardens and hosts workshops and tea tastings.

JOHNNY'S SELECTED SEEDS

877-564-6697

www.johnnyseeds.com

A respected supplier of seeds and tools since 1973. Sells a huge selection of organic, non-GMO seeds.

MOUNTAIN ROSE HERBS

541-741-7307

www.mountainroseherbs.com

Huge selection of bulk herbs (dried) and tea supplies.

RENEE'S GARDEN

888-880-7228

www.reneesgarden.com

Specializes in heirloom, non-GMO, organic seeds and open-pollinated varieties.

RICHTERS

800-668-4372

www.richters.com

Specializes in selling and shipping fresh herbs and herb seeds.

SEED SAVERS EXCHANGE

563-382-5990

www.seedsavers.org

Specializes in open-pollinated, heirloom seeds.

THE THYME GARDEN HERB COMPANY

541-487-8671

www.thymegarden.com

Offers herb seeds, dried herbs, and herbal tea blends.

ABOUT THE AUTHOR

Jodi Helmer is a North Carolina-based journalist who writes about food, gardening, farming, and the environment. She has written for *National Geographic Traveler, Hobby Farms, FarmLife, The Guardian, Smithsonian.com, Sierra.com,* and *Scientific American* and is the author of several books, including *Growing Your Own Tea Garden: The Guide to Growing and Harvesting Flavorful Teas in Your Backyard* and *Protecting Pollinators: How to Save the Creatures That Feed Our World.* When she's not writing, she works in the garden and raises bees.

PHOTO CREDITS

FC = front cover; BC = back cover; t = top; b = bottom; l = left; r = right; m = middle

The following images are credited to Shutterstock.com and their respective creators:
FC tl: Alexander Raths; FC bl: Nada Sertic; FC r: Chinara Guliyeva; BC t: LiliGraphie; BC bl: Oksana Mizina; BC br: Pixel-Shot; In Your Glass icon throughout: siaminka; 51–55 background: Pagina; 124–143 border illustration: notsoart; 1: Oleksandra Naumenko; 2: Petr Jilek; 4–5: Snowbelle; 6–7: Evgeny Karandaev; 8 t: HildaWeges Photography; 8 b: aliasemma; 9 t: food.kiro; 9 b: Charles Place; 10: sirtravelalot; 11: smirart; 12–13: etorres; 14 t: Evgeny Karandaev; 14 b: Alp Aksoy; 15 t: Everett Historical; 15 b: Katerinina; 16 t: Jake Hukee; 16 b: Katae.Olaree; 17 t: Natalia Klenova; 17 b: Brent Hofacker; 18: Odua Images; 19 t: baibaz; 20 b: GreenArt; 21 b: spatuletail; 22: zhu difeng; 23 t: Rajesh Narayanan; 24–25: Dani Vincek; 26 t: Carlos Rondon; 26 b: mizy; 27 t: marilyn barbone; 27 b: Manfred Ruckszio; 28 t: shansh23; 28 b: NazarPro; 29 t: SnelsonStock; 29 b: nnattalli; 30 t: ELAKSHI CREATIVE BUSINESS; 30 b: Sakcared; 31 t: emberiza; 31 b: Zigzag Mountain Art; 32 t: spline_x; 32 b: Przemyslaw Muszynski; 33 t: Aedka Studio; 33 b: 336food; 34 t: D_M; 34 b: Akvals; 35 t: Cozine; 35 b: simona pavan; 36 t: shansh23; 36 b: lzf; 37 t: PosiNote; 37 b: PosiNote; 38: Skyprayer2005; 38 b: Klemens Pohl; 39 t: Scisetti Alfio; 39 b: Martina Roth; 40 t: Aimmi; 40 b: Nannie_iiuu; 41 t: Scisetti Alfio; 41 b: JurateBuiviene; 42 t: Scisetti Alfio; 42 b: sasimoto; 43 t: Scisetti Alfio; 43 b: pkorchagina; 44 t: Scisetti Alfio; 44 b: Zigzag Mountain Art; 45 t: Martina Osmy; 45 b: Skyprayer2005; 46 t: Richard Peterson; 46 b: pilialoha; 47 t: Scisetti Alfio; 47 b: Ahmet Yasti; 48 t: anmbph; 48 b: ChWeiss; 49 t: Imageman; 49 b: waldenstroem; 50: Scisetti Alfio; 51 t: SOMMAI; 51 b: Lotus Images; 52: Maridav; 54: Iryna Denysova;

55: Nataliia Pyzhova; 56 t: Bjoern Wylezich; 56 b: NANCY AYUMI KUNIHIRO; 57 t: LianeM; 57 b: lightrain; 58 t: Marc Lee; 58 b: Gabriela Beres; 59 t: ZoranOrcik; 59 b: Africa Studio; 60 t: oksana2010; 60 b: Itija; 61: Scisetti Alfio; 62 t: spline_x; 62 b: Nada Sertic; 63 t: Scisetti Alfio; 63 b: Marques; 64 t: Scisetti Alfio; 64 b: Tukaram.Karve; 65 t: Hortimages; 65 b: dadalia; 66 t: Nyvlt-art; 66 b: Ezume Images; 67 t: Ziablik; 67 b: Grigorii Pisotsckii; 68 t: Gino Santa Maria; 68 b: Prokuronov Andrey; 69 t: kzww; 69 b: Anquetil Anthony; 70 t: Pingun; 70 b: Arina P Habich; 71 t: Swapan Photography; 71 b: Alter-ego; 72 t: Imageman; 72 b: Nick Pecker; 73 t: Wealthylady; 73 b: Menna; 74 t: Hong Vo; 74 b: Denise Lett; 75 t: anmbph; 75 b: yuris; 76 t: PIXbank CZ; 76 b: MityaC13; 77 t: Binh Thanh Bui; 77 b: Jen Wolf; 78 t: anmbph; 78 b: Matt Jones; 79 t: Santi S; 79 b: tmpr; 80 t: Manfred Ruckszio; 80 b: Volcko Mar; 81 t: photogal; 81 b: Jane McLoughlin; 82 t: Hortimages; 82 b: Manfred Ruckszio; 83 t: New Africa; 83 b: Denis Pogostin; 84 t: Ilizia; 84 b: De Jongh Photography; 85 t: ANGHI; 85 b: neil langan; 86: Mikhail Martynov; 87 t: Boonchuay1970; 87 b: Ihor Bondarenko; 88 t: Nata Studio; 88 b: Ihor Hvozdetskyi; 89 t: NUM LPPHOTO; 89 m: Picture Partners; 89 b: Doikanoy; 90 t: Jiang Zhongyan; 90 b: Igor Cheri; 91 t: limpido; 91 b: Manfred Ruckszio; 92 t: shansh23; 92 b: Ole Schoener; 93 t: Scisetti Alfio; 93 b: joloei; 94–95: Franz Peter Rudolf; 96 t: Yasonya; 96 bl: kryzhov; 96 br: richsouthwales; 97 t: Sergey Kamshylin; 97 b: Peter Turner Photography; 98 l: mythja; 98 r: Purino; 99 t: Four-leaf; 99 b: Jamie Hooper; 100 t: Christine Bird; 100 b: YuRi Photolife; 101 b: Rimma Bondarenko; 102 b: Anna Hoychuk; 103 b: Ievgeniia Maslovska; 104 b: Pat_Hastings; 105 b: Liliya Kandrashevich; 106 b: Martina Osmy; 107 b: Ivan Mateev; 108 b: Oksana Mizina; 109 b: George Dolgikh; 110–111: marcin jucha; 112 t: Vladimir Konstantinov; 112 b: samray; 113: Rawpixel.com; 114 t: Pixel-Shot; 114 mt: Proxima Studio; 114 mb: Fotobyjuliet; 114 b: July Prokopiv; 115 t: Niik Leuangboriboon; 115 mt: Evgeny Karandaev; 115 mm: Atsushi Hirao; 115 mb: Pixel-Shot; 115 b: Anna Hoychuk; 116 t: New Africa; 116 m: Andrey Arkusha; 116 b: Andrey Arkusha; 117 t: Andrey Arkusha; 117 mr: Andrey Arkusha; 117 ml: Andrey Arkusha; 117 b: Andrey Arkusha; 118: kazoka; 119 t: Geo-grafika; 119 b: Milante; 120 t: angelakatharina; 120 m: YURENIA NATALLIA; 120 b: julie deshaies; 121 t: Alexander Raths; 121 m: Kwang Meena; 121 b: Mariya Siyanko; 122–123: Liliya Kandrashevich; 124: Lyudmila Mikhailovskaya; 126 t: Stefano Cogliandro; 126 b: Maria Bry; 127: 5PH; 128 t: VICUSCHKA; 128 bl: Valentyn Volkov; 128 br: Dmity Trush; 129: Andrei Mayatnik; 130 t: Lea Brk; 130 b: Diana Taliun; 132: Brent Hofacker; 133 l: CHALERMCHAI99; 134: Evgeny Karandaev; 135: etorres; 136 r: Tim UR; 137: Candice Bell; 138: Alexey Lysenko; 139: Heike Rau; 140 t: StudioPhotoDFlorez; 140 b: Goskova Tatiana; 141 t: Viktor1; 141 b: Svittlana; 142 t: CWIS; 142 b: natashamam; 143: Aleksandr Lupin; 148: New Africa

The following images are credited to their respective creators: 23 b: Llara Pazdan; 53: JusTea; 101 t: Beth Kaiser; 102 t: Beth Kaiser; 103 t: Beth Kaiser; 104 t: Beth Kaiser; 105 t: Beth Kaiser; 106 t: Beth Kaiser; 107 t: Beth Kaiser; 108 t: Beth Kaiser; 109 t: Beth Kaiser; 131: Kyle Edwards; 133 r: Kyle Edwards; 136 l: Kyle Edwards; 144–145: United States Department of Agriculture (USDA), *https://planthardiness. ars.usda.gov*; 146–147: Natural Resources Canada, *www.planthardiness.gc.ca*; 149: Jodi Helmer

The following images are faithful photographic reproductions of two-dimensional works of art that are in the public domain in the United States, their countries of origin, and other countries depending on the copyright term: 19 b: page of *De Materia Medica*, dated circa 512, from the illuminated manuscript *Vienna Dioscurides*, author unknown; 20 l: painting titled "Portrait of a lady drinking tea," dated circa 1737–1807, by Niclas Lafrensen; 21 t: lithograph titled "The Destruction of Tea at Boston Harbor," dated 1846, by Nathaniel Currier

INDEX

Note: Page numbers in **bold** indicate plant primary discussions with "In Your Glass" recipes, and page numbers in *italics* indicate additional recipes.

A
alcohol-free drinks. *See* mocktails
anise hyssop, **26**
apple mint, **27**, 107

B
bearberry, **28**
bee balm, **29**, 104, *139*.
 See also lemon balm
beet, **70**, 102, *141*
bitters, about, 127
black currant, **72**
black tea, **54**, 118
blackberry, **71**, 126
blender, 114
blood orange, **73**, 108
brewing tea, 118
burdock, **87**

C
calendula, **59**, 109
Camellia sinensis, 19, 20, 22, **51**, **54**
cardamom, **30**
carrot, **74**, 102, *141*
catnip, **31**
celery, **75**, 86, 108
chamomile, **60**, 65, 92, 109, *125*
champagne flutes, 116
chemicals, avoiding, 112
chickweed, **32**, 112
chicory, **88**
chocolate mint, **33**
cilantro/coriander, **34**, 76
Citrus Lift Tea, *139*
Classic Cocktails Garden, 108
cocktails. *See also* making drinks;
 mocktails
 about: bitters primer, 127; gardens
 for ingredients. *See* garden
 designs; history and evolution of,
 14–18; mixing craft cocktails, 17;
 mocktails and, 17–18; overview
 of, 122
 Garden G and T, *137*
 Garden Margarita with
 Strawberries and Basil, *131*
 Garden Whiskey Sour with Egg
 White, *129*
 Hibiscus French 75, *128*
 Lavender Mojito, *134*
Mint Julep, *132*
Mojito, *133*
Red Sangria, *135*
Rhubarb Gimlet, *130*
Shrubs (overview, basic, hot-
 process, two-stage), *126–27*
Simple Syrups (basic, mint,
 lavender, rhubarb, hibiscus),
 124–25
Whiskey and Peaches, *136*
coriander. *See* cilantro/coriander
coupes, 116
cucumber, **76**, 105, 108, *137*
currant, black, **72**

D
dandelion, **61**, 112
dehydrating herbs, 119–20, 121
Drink Your Veggies Garden, 102
drying herbs, 119–20, 121

E
echinacea, **62**, 106, 109
Edible Flower Garden, 109
eucalyptus, **35**

F
fennel, **36**
flowers, types of. *See* ***Plant Index (p. 7)***;
 specific plants
French press, 114
Fruit Smoothie, *142*
fruits, types of. *See* ***Plant Index (p. 7)***;
 specific fruits

G
garden, creating
 about: approach to, 10–11;
 overview of, 94
 assessing location, 96–97
 avoiding chemicals, 112
 best practices, 96–99
 city/urban options, 100
 garden-to-glass and, 8–11
 harvesting and using
 your bounty, 11
 overharvesting precaution, 99
 pest control, 97–98
 safety disclaimer, 11
 soil preparation, 96
 structure considerations, 98–99
 tending plants, 97
garden designs, 101–9
 Classic Cocktails Garden, 108
 Drink Your Veggies Garden, 102
 Edible Flower Garden, 109
 Garnish Garden, 103
 H₂O Infusions Garden, 105
 Lemonade Stand Garden, 101
 Lovely Lemon Garden, 104
 Mint Medley Garden, 107
 Soothing Tea Garden, 106
Garden G and T, *137*
Garden Margarita with Strawberries
 and Basil, *131*
Garden Whiskey Sour with Egg
 White, *129*
Garnish Garden, 103
gimlet, rhubarb, *130*
gin and tonic, garden, *137*
ginger, 75, 79, **89**
ginseng, **90**
glassware, 116–18
green tea, **53**, 64, 118.
 See also yaupon
growing plants. *See* garden, creating

H
H₂O Infusions Garden, 105
harvesting ingredients
 following foraging laws, 113
 general guidelines, 11
 knowing what you pick, 112–13
 overharvesting precaution, 99
 storing/preserving/drying after,
 113, 119–20, 121
 tips for great beverages, 121
 washing after, 113
hibiscus, **63**
 Hibiscus French 75, *128*
 Hibiscus Simple Syrup, *125*
highball glasses, 117
history and evolution of cocktails,
 14–18
history of tea, 19–22
holy basil, **37**

I
Infused Water, *143*. *See also* H₂O
 Infusions Garden

J

jasmine, **64**

juicer/juice press, 114

K

kale, **77**, 102

kettle, 114

L

lavender, **65**, 103, 105, 106

    Lavender Lemonade, *140*

    Lavender Mojito, *134*

    Lavender Simple Syrup, *125*

    Mmm Mint Iced Tea, *138*

lavender mint, **38**, 103, *138*

leaves, types of.

    *See **Plant Index (p. 7)**; specific plants*

lemon. *See* Meyer lemon

lemon balm, **39**, 60, 61, 104, *139*

lemon garden design, 104

lemon verbena, **41**, 60, 62, 104, 106, *125*, *129*, *139*

Lemonade Stand Garden, 101

lemongrass, **40**

licorice, **91**. *See also* anise hyssop; fennel; holy basil

M

making drinks. *See also* cocktails; harvesting ingredients; mocktails

    about: overview of, 110, 112–13

    cleaning equipment, 113

    harvesting ingredients and, 11, 112–13

    tips for great beverages, 121

    tools for, 114–15

margarita glasses, 117

margarita with strawberries and basil, *131*

marjoram, **42**

martini glasses, 117

measuring cups, 115

Meyer lemon, **78**, *140*, *141*, *143*

mint, types of. *See* apple mint; chocolate mint; lavender mint; peppermint; spearmint

Mint Julep, *132*

Mint Medley Garden, 107

Mint Simple Syrup, *125*

mocktails. *See also* making drinks

    about: evolution of, 17–18; making, 126

    Citrus Lift Tea, *139*

    Fruit Smoothie, *142*

    Infused Water, *143*

    Lavender Lemonade, *140*

    Mmm Mint Iced Tea, *138*

    Veggie Juice, *141*

Mojitos, *133*, *134*

mortar and pestle, 115

O

oolong tea, **55**, 118

P

parsley, **43**, *103*

peaches, whiskey and, *136*

peppermint, **44**, 101, 106, 107, 108, *138*

persimmons, **79**

pest control, 97–98

pineapple sage, **45**, *129*

plant hardiness zone maps, 21, 144–47

plants, choosing, 20–21.

    *See also **Plant Index (p. 7)**; specific plants*

preserving harvest after (drying/dehydrating), 119–20, 121

purple passionflower, **66**, 109

R

raspberry, **80**, 108

recipes. *See* cocktails; mocktails

red clover, **67**

Red Sangria, *135*

resources, 148

rhubarb, **81**

    Rhubarb Gimlet, *130*

    Rhubarb Simple Syrup, *125*

rocks glasses, 117

roots, types of. *See **Plant Index (p. 7)**; specific plants*

rose, rugosa, **82**

rosemary, **46**, 96

rugosa rose, **82**

S

sage, **47**. *See also* pineapple sage

sangria, red, *135*

shakers, 115

Shrubs (overview, basic, hot-process, two-stage), 126–27

sieves, 115

Simple Syrups (basic, mint, lavender, rhubarb, hibiscus), 124–25

smoothie, fruit, *142*

soil preparation, 96

Soothing Tea Garden, 106

spearmint, **48**, 105, 107, *132*, *138*

spinach, **83**, 102

St. John's wort, **50**

staghorn sumac, **84**

stevia, growing, **93**

stinging nettle, **49**

storing dried herbs, 113, 119–20

strawberry, **85**, 101, 103, 105, *131*, *142*, *143*

T

tea

    brewing guidelines by type, 118

    Camellia sinensis, 19, 20, 22, **51**, **54**

    finances associated with, 22–23

    history of, 19–22

    Soothing Tea Garden, 106

    tisanes and, 20

tea plant. *See* black tea; *Camellia sinensis*; green tea; oolong tea; white tea

tea-ball strainer, 115

thyme, **56**, 104, 126

tisanes, 20, 118

tomato, **86**, 102

tools for making drinks, 114–15. *See also* glassware

trumpet honeysuckle, **68**, 109

tufted violet, **69**

U

urban gardens, 100

V

valerian, **92**

vegetable garden design, 102

vegetables, types of.

    *See **Plant Index (p. 7)**; specific vegetables*

Veggie Juice, *141*

violet. *See* tufted violet

W

water, infused, *143*. *See also* H_2O Infusions Garden

Whiskey and Peaches, *136*

whiskey sour with egg white, garden, *129*

white tea, **52**, 118

wine, in Red Sangria, *135*

witch hazel, **57**

Y

yaupon, **58**